D1607894

THE COURAGE MACHINE

THE COURAGE MACHINE
A New Life in a New World

Souvenirs: Volume II
Translated by Margaret Anderson and Solita Solano

Georgette Leblanc

Book Studio 2012

Originally published as *La Machine à Courage: Souvenirs* by J. B. Janin, 1947

ISBN: 978-0-9559090-7-8

Cover: Drawing of Georgette Leblanc by Djuna Barnes, 1920,
courtesy of the Library of Congress.

British Library Cataloguing-in-Publication Data.
A catalogue record for this book is available from the British Library.

I dedicate this book to Friendship—
the strength and sweetness of life . . .
to all-powerful, thrice-blest Friendship.

G. L.

CONTENTS

PREFACE

WHAT a magnificent title! The only one that expresses this astonishing woman whom we mourn.

Reading this title, I see her equipped with wheels and hands of mystery like the mechanisms of Ezekiel's dream; whirring wheels, tongues of fire, hands, wings, exploding stars. And this incomprehensible machine thunders and flames in order to produce courage, sacks of courage, bales of courage, miles of courage, masses of that courage with which man defies destiny and by which he changes the lines in his hand.

Hers was a great epoch. In it there still existed those superstars who scorn public opinion, who do not even know it exists, and who move through the crowd, headless and armless, propelled only by the power of their souls, as immutable as the Victory of Samothrace.

How can ordinary women, dreaming of fashion and furniture, prevail against the winds of fate?

Georgette rode a bicycle in a lace dress, under a burning sky, up and down dusty hills in the train of the tireless Maeterlinck.

Like Phèdre, piercing the laurel with her golden pin, she hid in the groves and overheard the bargainings of life. To her they were incredible. She braved ruin and disaster. Her goal was the great glory, the terrible battle of the angel: to resist the temptations of beauty.

Always along her way she found companions who cherished her, protected her and made her task a little easier. But she was alone. Alone she was born. Alone she lived. Alone she died. She was to furnish a model for a saint of lyricism.

Where one lives—does it matter? She lived in soul-destroying villas, cruel hotels, abandoned lighthouses. From morning to night her trailing gown swept aside the dead leaves of daily events. Her inner goal was little concerned with these sweepings.

She strode ahead. She advanced, she challenged, she sought to convince, she struggled. She met ingratitude, laughter, the silence of hard hearts. She was a courage-machine, fed by a secret electricity. I lift a smoke-screen, such as conceals the movements of ships.

Unseen, all-seeing, slow and yet swifter than lightning, she disrupted the traffic—that quadrille danced by solemn feet, in which the pre-arranged patterns do not admit of the slightest disorder. Georgette was disorder itself—the disorder that rejects dead order. It was order of a kind—*her* order, the order dictated by her voices. The order that kills.

It is impossible to think of her without evoking the legend of the Phoenix. She flutters her vivid feathers. She sends forth her cry. She touches a flame to the pyre, mounts it and is consumed. Her ashes vibrate. In them she finds the force with which to reinvent her substance.

Who tells us she is dead? Death has little power over a courage-machine. Georgette is born again from her ashes. In her cloud of smoke we see her regain her lovely form and, with wings thundering, spring with a great cry straight into the heaven of high enterprise.

Ever faithful to our rendezvous.

Jean Cocteau
Paris, October 1945

FOREWORD

OUR planet today is covered with courage-machines. This prompts me to explain—to excuse, rather—the title of this second book of "Souvenirs."

To begin with, the title is not for myself alone. It applies to the lives of all artists. When I say "artist" I mean something outdated—that romantic race destined to disappear in a world which I have always called the "material-world." I belong to this race. It is a misfortune and it is all the beatitudes. It means that one has a thousand palettes with which to taste to the utmost the delights of life.

If I were to define my life in a word I would call it a quest. A quest of what? One needs almost a lifetime to answer this question.

First of all I searched for life through what is called "living." But I always felt that "life" is not there where we are, nor in the events which happen to us. Where is it? I searched and searched. By force of searching I found myself in darkness. I stayed there a long time . . . I might say—nowhere; having lost everything and not yet having found anything. Between what one no longer accepts and what one hopes for there is a void. Little by little all became clear.

The writing of "The Courage Machine," which covers ten years, was retarded by illness. For a long time I lived beside death. But I had a presentiment that something essential—something foreseen in New York—would develop for me during these last years. I was not mistaken.

Between my life in America and that of today an enormous space stretches. It is because the years from fifty to sixty count double—one has kept what one had and gained what one did not have. This book follows an evolution which, for me, is not a curve but an ascending line. There is a beginning and an end;

a new beginning, an advance, and a new search; then again an advance—but this time on an essential plane, where the great events are inner ones.

Georgette Leblanc

CHAPTER ONE
A NEW WORLD

1919. I stood on Brooklyn Bridge in New York. A hard wind was beating against me and I held my coat with both hands to protect my body. A body was all I possessed—nothing when you have everything, everything when you have nothing.

I had been wandering among giant things. Now I watched the crowd hurry across the bridge. I did not understand its intentions, I did not understand its words. From a distance I stared at the extraordinary city. Through the bridge's cables on that white winter morning its spires and towers looked like chessmen for Titans.

In my purse I carried the number of the bus that would take me back to the hotel. I felt absolutely free, free even of myself, without a name and without a language. And I was trying to be without a past.

The bus from the bridge left me in front of the Madison Square Hotel where Monique and I had been staying since our arrival from France a few days before. Throwing down her sewing, losing her glasses, she rushed to me—"How are you, chérie?" Today as in the past, this is the way she always welcomes me. Whether I have crossed the garden or the Atlantic, her anxious voice questions me with the same solicitude.

As she took my coat Monique announced good news. One of the newspaper editors, a friend of Véral D., had found us an apartment where we could live for "almost nothing." "Those newspaper men are so good," she added, "they will tell us everything we are expected to do."

I remembered Véral's last words in Paris: "In America I will direct your affairs in a completely new manner, according to my system of explosion." But on the boat I had received a cable from him: "Keep arrival strictly incognito." I knew enough of

American ways and the enormous importance given to the arrival of celebrities to be surprised at such a request. However, as we approached the Statue of Liberty I obeyed the cable, covered my face with a heavy veil and watched reporters swarm over the decks. They finally found Monique's cabin. Monique is a poor liar and kept repeating, "I don't know Georgette Leblanc, I don't know her." These blushing denials only enlivened the reporters and at last they tracked me down. "You are Georgette Leblanc!" In despair I cried, "I don't know." To escape the cameras I fled up and down corridors and hid in a bathroom. I was carrying my fish, St. Augustine, in his bowl under my cape, and when I looked in at him I saw the little flame writhing in his glass prison, almost dry. Monique found me as I was bringing him back to life under water. "Ah, ma petite chérie, what an adventure; I lied very well but those men are clever. There is no way of hiding anything from them."

Since my arrival I had been waiting to hear when the *Sunday American* intended to publish my memoirs. But Véral said, "Don't be impatient, you must think only of being happy, we will take care of business while you go sightseeing." After my experiences of the last two years, nothing could have pleased me more than this life in parentheses; perhaps a little too much . . . Véral's eyes were without guile and his standardized smile was paternal. He was sure of himself—like all those who, having nothing, have nothing to lose. He inspired confidence—an indispensable quality for those who live by their wits.

Late that evening we went with him to see the apartment. A large perfumed lady received us in a Japanese kimono, but I gave no attention to her or to the apartment—I was hypnotized by the sight of a grand piano that occupied half of the living-room and I saw everything in terms of it.

When I was asked to pay four months' rent in advance—one thousand dollars—I protested, but my manager interrupted:

"The newspaper will pay half."

"But why?"

"Because that's the arrangement in your contract."

We strolled home along Broadway, beneath celestial and commercial fireworks. A procession of clowns leaping at the sky advertised a chewing-gum; the glory of a famous mineral water blazed through a spray of sparkling rockets; a sapphire dragon blew forth a fountain of youth of an offensive red. All the cardinal points spat folly at the dead stars and the spent moon.

As we walked I asked Véral, "What have you planned for me?" My unfathomable manager smiled. "First of all we are going to hide you." Then he explained his system of explosion. "In America success depends upon surprise—you have to explode like a bomb. You are lucky to be with the *Sunday American*, one of the biggest newspapers in the country, and the editors are interested in your success. The moment your memoirs appear we will arrange your debut—you'll sing, act, lecture, make a film, all at once. It will be magnificent!"

Véral shone with enthusiasm. Hat in hand, he offered his bald crown to Broadway's colored lights and walked beside me like a conqueror.

"You can't imagine the vastness of our plans! Novelty is what counts. In your case it's going to be mystery, mystery, and then . . ."

He stopped and flung up his arms. A spray of golden rockets burst in the sky and at the top of his lungs he yelled, "explosion!"

The next night there was a deluge. While thunder fell in colonnades we moved to the new apartment. Véral rode in the taxi with St. Augustine and me and I watched his sulky Roman profile reflected in the glass window. My fish was the cause of his hostility—"You'll find hundreds like it anywhere," he said. The bowl was balanced on my knees and in revenge I let the water splash on him at every turning.

We were greeted by a flash of joy in the black face of the doorman. He waved his great hands over St. Augustine—"Hello, boy! Hello, French fish! How do you do?"

The elevator that took us up seemed to mount by our happiness alone . . . And then, after Véral had left, we discovered our mistake. Everything was dusty and in disorder; the furniture was dilapidated and unsteady; after investigating the beds we dared not sleep in them. We installed ourselves in armchairs for the night, counting the hours and waiting for morning. It never came, and I realized why when I went to the window at nine o'clock—the wall of the building opposite us was so close that I could almost touch it. Above my head, as if at the end of a long vertical corridor, I saw a small space of grey sky and breathed a poisonous reek from a restaurant which opened on the narrow court below. I shut the window, turned on the light, and remembered that I had paid four months' rent.

Véral was called to the rescue. He suggested extravagant and impossible ways of freeing me immediately from my lease, but the woman who had rented us the apartment had left for an unknown destination. I discovered several months later that she was the mistress of one of the newspaper men.

One day Véral took me to the offices of the *Sunday American*. The building—a long façade of dark walls and small windows—made me think of prison. All the editors of the paper were introduced to me, but when I asked to meet the owner, William Randolph Hearst, everyone laughed. I was told that he never came here; that he owned several newspapers and lived in several countries at once.

The business manager, Mr. Read, who soon was to play the principal role in my affairs, was a man of forty who looked sixty. He had the head of a skinned fox, a yellow face, and a coat too wide for his thin shoulders. His pale bored eyes were like panes of glass with a perpetual rain behind them; when he was pleased, the rain lifted enough for a beam of sunlight to filter through

the lids. He went to church on Sunday with his wife, a vast creature with flat feet, dressed in black satin adorned with jade. The
editor-in-chief looked and acted like a wild boar. Completing the
group with which I was to be surrounded were the Smiths—he
a wily biped, she built like a quadruped, low to the ground, mas-
sive, powerful.

If I had not been living in a sort of lethargy I would never have
allowed such a group of people to take charge of my affairs. As it
was, I scarcely listened to their talk, I was elsewhere. I was neither
happy nor unhappy. I did not know toward what I was going,
while waiting for the source of a real life to come to me, I merely
thought, "What does life, all-powerful life, want of me? Why am
I like a winter field, and when will spring return?"

Although I knew a few people in New York I refrained from
telephoning them. "Don't let anyone know you are here," said
Véral, "until you have made your first appearance."

Every day I went out alone, walking at random and looking
at everything—my days were spent in looking. I went everywhere my curiosity drew me and it led me one day to the very
top of the famous old Hippodrome. Through an alley I saw a
wide iron stairway and started up it, climbing flight after flight
until I opened a door and found myself in the last row of an immense amphitheater. Far below I saw a brilliant stream of clowns,
horses, flags—a sparkling phantasmagoria, I was too high above
the stage to see the performance clearly, but I was fascinated by
the audience—living walls made of clapping hands and howling
mouths. Here was the enthusiasm of the American race in action—that race, composed of the most audacious and vigorous
elements of all the other nations of the world.

And then, upon the delirious arena, a total and trembling silence fell, as if the audience were holding its breath. It made me
think of the silence of a forest, at night, when one suddenly becomes aware of the breathing of the earth. The brutality of the

projectors was dimmed, and after a pause a slender black silhouette made its way to the footlights. A translucent voice floated up to the galleries, its exquisite notes like the flowering of skyrockets against a dark night-sky. A religious peace spread over the arena ... When the song was over the reaction of the audience surpassed even my expectation. A chorus of mad and frenzied cries mounted to the roof ... I felt the boiling-up of those forces which I would soon be facing myself, and I rushed home to tell Monique how right we had been to come to this vital land.

Time passes quickly when it is not used. The days marked only by my sight-seeing promenades, flowed away like hours. Every time I asked Véral when this aimless existence would end he always answered, "Don't try to hurry destiny." He even thought it unimportant that the English translation of my memoirs was not yet finished. I continued to walk and wait.

We soon found a way to compensate for the daytime darkness of our apartment. Many houses in New York have flat roofs—ours was a black terrace, surrounded by old chimneys and piles of fire hose. Nevertheless the place was my delight. I went there early in the morning when smoke from the chimneys rose gently upward; I went there in the afternoon before the day faded; Monique and I had our tea there as the sun went down. But we missed the pink twilights of Paris and those suspended moments that separate day from darkness. In New York the beauty that comes at the day's end is broken by artificial light. When electric beams began to streak across the sky, Monique and I descended the narrow iron stairway.

One day I received word from the newspaper that the translation of my memoirs was finished, but Véral and Read came to tell me that slight changes in the text were necessary. "I'll change anything you like," I said. "Tell me what I should do."

"You don't have to change anything," said Mr. Read, "we've done it for you."

"But I stipulated that nothing could be changed, or added, without my consent."

Read said, "You don't understand the psychology of the American public. You must give us a free hand with the changes."

"Only if I approve of them," I said.

They realized that I could not be moved and at last agreed to show me what they had written into my manuscript.

Although, we lived carefully, our simple needs were more than we could afford. I possessed neither money nor jewels when I left France. What I had earned there in the last years by producing Maeterlinck's plays I had used to present other beautiful and little-known dramas; and during the war, like everyone else, I had made no money. Of course I could have had a little foresight, but to me, foresight is premeditated avarice.

The *Sunday American* showed me their "improvements" in my manuscript. They were of a sensational inaccuracy that I was forced to reject.

Every night Véral telephoned to say, "I am here, ma chère, sleep in peace. I am letting it be whispered about that you are in New York, mystery surrounds you, curiosity is awakening."

Each week he drew a small sum from the newspaper for us to live on. Then suddenly he "forgot" to bring it to us. We waited for him from day to day, but he never came. When he finally reappeared it was to announce that the *Sunday American* refused to continue its advances unless I agreed to the revisions of the manuscript. "But I have a contract," I said, "the paper has only to publish and pay me." "That would have been done long since," Véral said, "if they were free. But since you don't accept the paper's point of view, the publication can drag along indefinitely—for months, even years. In fact, they can refuse to publish you at all."

A band tightened around my throat.

"In which case," Véral continued, "all you have to do is to repay the paper and take back your book."

When I didn't answer he made a final appeal: "You are refusing a fortune. One doesn't refuse a fortune!"

A day or two later he and Read came together to persuade me. What they called the "sensationalism indispensable to the American reader," I called the most outrageous vulgarity. There remained for me only the right to refuse. It was my only weapon but I would use it to the end, whatever the cost.

"Don't you realize," they pleaded, "that you are throwing away thousands of dollars? This isn't a question of literature, this is a business affair."

"It would be too sad," I said, "if a sublime human experience should become only a business affair."

They finally left, defeated. In our little salon, dark at three o'clock, Monique held my hands and leaned on my shoulder. "What will become of us, chérie?"

In New York artists without money are like whirling dervishes, who turn forever in a frenzy of hopeless plans. I was asked to do "Pelléas and Mélisande" in English and I worked night and day to master the text; but when I was ready there wasn't enough money for the production. A Frenchwoman wanted to arrange a series of French concerts—she knew of a millionaire who might be interested in such a venture; but after all the details had been arranged she arrived at our door one morning, breathless, to tell me that the millionaire's house was surrounded by police—he was a common crook. A Hollywood film company telephoned me a dazzling offer to star in a picture, "What kind of picture?" I asked. "Your life with Maeterlinck. Everything for you, everything against Maeterlinck." I hung up.

Véral tried in vain to find financial backing for a concert or a play. He took me to see theatrical managers, expecting me to convince and conquer. Not speaking English and having no conquering clothes, I was not equipped for such a role. During this time my manuscript was still being discussed. The editors refused to show me their alterations and suggested that I myself add new material. I feverishly produced stories of the theatre and amusing personal anecdotes but the editors rejected them—only a sensational version of my life with Maeterlinck would satisfy them.

Véral thought of a new idea. "You can make a thousand dollars a week in vaudeville," he said. "I know a real poet who will write you a sketch." When the masterpiece was finished Véral brought it to me in all confidence and sat before me as I read it. It was called "The Golden Bird" and the setting was a study in an abbey:

A poet, made up to resemble Maeterlinck, meditates at his desk. He invokes the ceiling for inspiration which does not come. The door opens and I appear, dressed in gold. To encourage genius, I go into plastic poses. The poet poises his pen but writes nothing. I disappear. A young serving-maid enters. She is called Cerisette, the name of an apéritif supposed to excite inspiration. She runs to a cupboard, brings forth a bottle and gives the poet a drink. He begins to write, one eye on his work, the other on the friskings of the maid. Genius is resurrected. At this point I return, still a gold statue, and symbolize renouncement by carrying a travelling bag. We exchange dramatic gestures. The action grows swifter. Another bottle, and the poet reels. A shining stairway is lowered. The Golden Bird climbs upward, singing a hymn of peace, while the other two move toward an alcove in which can be seen a couch and a bar. The curtain falls.

Startled by my anger, Véral began to believe that he had exhausted his possibilities.

"Monna Vanna"

We didn't go out any more—fresh air sharpens the appetite. I noticed signs of depletion in Monique that filled me with anxiety. One night when we were dining as usual on milk and apples, I suddenly thought of a solution for our desperate situation. I put

A NEW WORLD

on an evening dress and asked Monique to bring me my chinchilla cape. "I have a plan," I said, "I'm going to the Chicago Opera."

"Mon Dieu!" she cried, "you're not going to hear 'Monna Vanna'?" "Yes," I said, "tonight 'Monna Vanna' doesn't matter."

At the opera I went directly to the box of Madame Oscar Hammerstein who had invited me to come whenever I liked —she
was managing the Manhattan Opera Company since the death
of her husband. As I was knocking at the door, a young man came
out of the adjoining box and bowed to me. I didn't recognize
him but returned his greeting. Madame Hammerstein drew me
in, presented her guests and seated me beside her. The opera had
begun and Mary Garden was already on the stage.

As soon as the curtain fell, the young man who had bowed to
me came to introduce himself. His name was Allen Tanner. He
spoke a French of his own invention, but I was able to understand that he had met me when I was playing "Monna Vanna" in
Boston in 1912. He had a sensitive nervous face and long slender
hands of which he seemed perpetually conscious. He told me
that he was a pianist and that he lived only "*dans le piano.*"

The curtain rose on the tent scene, with Muratore singing
Prinzivalle. Feeling less sad, I closed my eyes and rested in the
vibrations of the music—Garden, enveloped in cool veils, didn't
evoke Vanna for me. But the end of the act roused me—the
clamor of bells, the shouting, the triumphant cries, all the excitement of sound which I myself had directed so many times in so
many theatres . . . I sat transfixed by the pain of the past until the
voice of Madame Hammerstein recalled me. "Will you come
backstage and speak to Garden?" I powdered my face and rose
automatically.

Garden's dressing-room was crowded. Over the massed shoulders and heads I caught sight of the turban which framed her
strong and beautiful face. Suddenly the crowd parted and she
cried, "Georgette Leblanc!" Before I could speak she hurried on,
"How did you like the orchestra, and the sets? And the singing?

This isn't the first time you've been in New York? I'm singing "Thaïs" next week, you must come . . ."

I forced my way out against a stream of new arrivals. As I walked through the lobby a tall pier glass reflected my approach in an image larger than myself. It seemed to be holding my dead life in its arms.

I went to Muratore's dressing-room. He saw me in the crowd and with a sweeping gesture cried, "Make room for Monna Vanna!" Then, "Why haven't we heard you yet in New York? Who is your manager?" I explained my difficulties with the *Sunday American* and he shook his head. "Alas, if I weren't leaving how I would love to help you!"

The third act ended, the audience left, Madame Hammerstein and I stayed behind in the darkened theatre at the foot of the grand staircase. Her face was gentle, her eyes soft, I told her of my difficulties and she pressed my hands in sympathy. Then I asked the question that I had come to ask—would she buy my chinchilla cape?

She sank down on the stairs and began to weep. She had no money, only overwhelming debts—her jewels were sold, her theatre mortgaged and the box-office receipts seized every night. Facing dire poverty, she thought only of suicide. It was I who consoled her.

The next day I received a bouquet of Japanese lilies and a letter from Allen Tanner. I copy the letter textually:

Chère Madame,

A coups de dictionnaire, je m'assis vous écrire. A dire la vé-
rité, je n'ai jamais été présenté à vous. Je me suis présenter au
grand besoin me contenter à cause d'une admiration profonde,
laquelle a exister toute ma vie. Pardonnez-moi. Ne croyez pas
que je suis présomptueux: il fallait vous addresser parce que

c'est un visage telement me connaître, telement admiré et telement sympathique.

Je suis musicien, dévoué à Debussy, Ravel, Scriabin et tous
les vrais magiciens. Voulez-vous être si gentil, me permetter
vous voir, chère Madame? Peut-être nous pouvons faire la mu-
sique.

A bientôt, j'espère.

Allen Tanner

I thanked him by telephone. His comic French gave me a gig-
gle.

"Aoh! You will teach me?"

"Never, your language is too amusing!"

We arranged that he should come to tea that afternoon.

He came, bringing touching little presents wrapped in gold
paper—maple sugar, sweet biscuits and cocoa. "They are American specialties," he said. His voice was low and sounded like a bell
softly rung. "You sing, of course?" I asked. "Oh yes," he said, like
a child, "you will see."

It was a lovely day and we went up to the roof. Life was suddenly so changed that I took the three flights at a run. For nearly four months I had been associating with businessmen, all of
them stamped with that heavy puerility which anchors life to the
ground. Now for the first time I had met a young American, an
artist, intelligent, enthusiastic, articulate. Allen talked of music,
books and painting, of his long admiration for me, of the photographs he had collected of St. Wandrille, "Pelléas" and "Macbeth." And then he told me a little story. On Christmas day while
walking along Sixth Avenue, profiting from the roar of the el-
evated trains to sing "Pelléas" in full voice, he had seen a woman
wrapped in a leopard coat and veils coming out of a Child's restaurant. He knew it was I even without seeing my features. He
was too shy to speak to me but he rushed to his friends on Eighth

Street crying, "Georgette Leblanc is in New York, I have seen her!" They had been waiting to see me ever since.

I well-remembered that Christmas day. Monique and I had stopped before a sparkling white restaurant to read the sign in the window—"Ladies Invited." What an extraordinary country, I thought, and hurried Monique in for a free Christmas feast. We ordered everything on the menu and ate for an hour. Finally a waiter approached, beaming with Christmas cheer but presenting a bill. I explained our mistake to the manager who, fortunately, had no doubts of our naïveté. He told us the sign only meant that ladies were welcome. We gave him the few pennies we had and he accepted our promise to return and pay the rest as soon as possible.

In his fantastic French, Allen told me of his friends on Eighth Street, Margaret Anderson and Jane Heap. In the summer, he said, they lived in a wild place, near the sea, where there were no roads, nothing but trees; they had built their house themselves and even made their own furniture. Listening to his extraordinary descriptions, I pictured two prehistoric creatures brandishing axes in the woods, building their hut, sleeping on planks, living on roots and leaves. "But what do they do in winter?" I asked. "Oh, in winter they come to New York." They were two intellectuals and published an art magazine!

Allen lived with a musician friend in a studio apartment of the "Beaux Arts." His mother lived in the Middle West. He loved and admired her because she was brave. During thunder storms she always stood on a balcony, with lightning flashing all around her. I was almost ill from laughter.

As Allen talked he leaned against the railing, his elbows thrown back, his long hands hanging from his supple wrists. I was eager to see how they would touch a piano. We went downstairs and he played Bach, Chopin, Debussy, Scriabin. From the first note I recognized that lyrical musicality which is born and cannot be acquired; and when I sang for him he accompanied me with the inspired rhythms that belong to composers. An enchanting perspective opened before me with Allen's arrival in my life. I thanked him.

But in a few days he left for Chicago, to be gone for a month, and another interlude of solitude and poverty lay before us. Monique was able to obtain milk and fruit, sometimes two little rolls on credit from the friendly grocer's around the corner. Our daily life was hidden from the world. I was determined that my family in France should know nothing of my situation. They would urge me to return and that was a solution I would not admit, knowing that if I left the country my manuscript would be published in scandalous form and content.

Monique, wiser than I, occupied herself with sewing while I walked the floor, searching for a solution in a brain that rocked like a boat. Time was passing and I had the sensation that everything was falling away from me. It was really my life that was falling. I saw everything through a haze, I didn't understand what was said to me, I could not think. Something was pulling me down and I could no longer struggle against it. That something was hunger.

I went to consult a lawyer, a friend of Madame Hammerstein. He was very busy and as he didn't want to keep me waiting asked if he might lunch while we talked. The tray was on his desk, I sat close to the smell of toast, coffee, eggs, bacon. I told my story automatically, going into great detail, concentrating on my choice of words as if I no longer knew my own language. My hand was lying on the corner of the desk and I noticed that it was touching the corner of the tray as if about to take something. I stared at it as if it were a hand that didn't belong to me; it belonged only to a body that was hungry. Blushing, I replaced it in my lap. The lawyer advised me to submit my memoirs to Dodd, Mead and Company, who had already published three of my books.

I went to see Mr. Dodd and in my memory he is rose-colored; not only because I identify him with a special felicity, but because he was made of the colors of dawn—a young girl's complexion, corn-colored hair, yellow tortoise-shell glasses and the vibrations of a spring morning. He quickly agreed to publish my book after its appearance in the *Sunday American*, but on one condition: he had been Maeterlinck's publisher for many years and could not risk displeasing him; therefore his decision must wait until after he had read the manuscript.

When I saw him the next day his glasses grew misty and he stammered out that I had written a "pious book." And when I told him of my struggles with the newspaper editors his eyes overflowed and he blew his nose with abandon. His partner came in and gravely shook my hand. Deeply affected by so much sympathy, I was seized with a great pity for myself.

Mr. Dodd gave me a check for a thousand dollars and pronounced a few solemn words which lent a sacred quality to the transaction. It was agreed that the shocking translation made by the *Sunday American* would be destroyed and a new one made by Véral.

As soon as we left the Dodd Mead office Véral said, "Since I am to do the translation, may I have my five hundred in advance? My wife and children are in terrible distress and this will save their lives." Like all emotional people, my judgment is unbalanced. I gave him the five hundred, but he never did the translation and, as I learned later, his wife never received any of the money.

Dazed by riches, we moved to a new setting—the Commodore Hotel. We took a sitting-room on the twenty-first floor, with two narrow beds hidden in alcoves. Our immense window enchanted my lungs—nothing limited the view over a field of roofs and chimneys. But such brightness required flowers. I went out and brought back, pressed to my heart, three little pots of red tulips.

A woman was waiting to see me. She looked like a provincial spinster of the 1890s. Her hair was arranged in neat sausages which served as a pedestal for a perky little hat, aggressively green, with an aigrette in front and a rose at the side. Beneath a chocolate-colored suit trimmed with braid, a merciless corset bound an allegorical bosom. This abundant person who should have presented me with a horn of plenty, held a small roll of paper which she twisted nervously under the sheltering balcony of her opulence.

In an ingenious voice and in perfect French she said, "I am from the *Evening World* and I've come to interview you. I chiefly do interviews on love." She paused to blush. "You see, that's my specialty." She gave a jubilant little laugh, put on her glasses and read aloud her questionnaire:

1. How does one distinguish between true and false love?
2. Should a man have two loves in his life to acquire experience?
3. What should one do if one loves without being loved?
4. What should the abandoned victim of love do?
5. Why doesn't love last forever?
6. Can a woman love after forty?
7. What is a great love?
8. What makes a great lover?

As I sat watching this exhibition of incredible naïveté I did not even feel an impulse to laugh.

I soon learned that my interviewer did not have, as she claimed, a monopoly on the subject of love. Other reporters besieged me with the same questions in the belief that a Frenchwoman has conclusive verdicts on all love's problems.

Love in America is a sort of clandestine mystery. One woman said to me, "Before my marriage I knew nothing, but afterward . . . !" and her eyes closed in gratitude to the universe. A young bride, a musician, told me that she had married for the sake of her art.

"Ah?" I said.

"Yes, I play the violin. My teacher said, 'You can't make any further progress as long as you don't know life. You must marry!' So I did. Now my playing is all changed because I know life."

I looked at her—short hair, flat chest, a face like an apple, a little shiny nose, the astringent voice of an adolescent, an ardor like that of a child before a candy-shop. Evidently this young person had been the object of a revelation.

Then the young husband appeared. "Hello! Hello!" he called, and with a heavy hand patted his wife's shoulder. He was a handsome boy, made for sports, too tall, too wide, with arms so long that they didn't know what to do when they had nothing to do. So this was the magician-hero. A night in his arms and the cosmos held no further secrets.

By now I had discarded the order to remain in hiding and was seeing the friends from whom I had hidden my arrival. They understood my scruples about the *Sunday American* but saw no solution. Their advice was: "You are involved with a formidable power, you won't be able to extricate yourself. Just make money and don't worry about anything else." And they added, "Four months of doing nothing in New York—you are already lost."

CHAPTER TWO
DEFEAT IN VICTORY

IT was spring. Monique and I had walked in the new sun to Central Park to be close to the earth. I breathed it in, closing my eyes. Spring is the same everywhere.

We sat on the grass to eat our lunch—bread and a bar of chocolate. The air was still, the sky without a flaw; not far away in their iron cages the wild beasts slept, innocent and rich. The angelus is not rung in America, but by the expression of the earth I knew that it was midday. Birds were singing faintly in the quiet trees.

I threw myself back on the grass. "How happy we are, Monique, how happy we are!"

On the evening of that first spring day, Allen asked me to come down to the lobby of the Commodore where Margaret Anderson was waiting to meet me. As I stepped out of the elevator I saw a sky-blue silhouette, a white glove waving and a lovely smile of welcome beneath a fur toque. Two sky-blue arms opened and we embraced, each leaving on the cheek of the other a tiny red spot. It was as if we had always known each other.

As we started out for the Park I began to laugh so breathlessly that we had to stop walking. The extreme chic of Margaret's suit, her beauty and elegance . . . and the prehistoric woman of Allen's stories! Without understanding why, they laughed with me. Margaret had bursts of clear silver laughter, but she spoke in a contralto voice of throaty notes. What interested me above all was the way she looked out from her eyes, set in orbits of perfect design; when she was silent their color deepened and they became innocently meditative like those of a baby. Her light way of walking made her seem propelled by emotion. Her gestures were original: she had an amusing way of thrusting out her left elbow and holding it high, her hand against her breast, the fingers widely separated.

She spoke no French and I no English, but there was no barrier between us. The intensity which characterized her needed no words to find and join my own. When she argued, her eyes were no longer ingenuous but filled with convictions which transported her. Momentum, intensity, conviction are the words which describe my first impression of her. And total simplicity.

There are few words more abused in their meaning than the word "simplicity." A woman is called simple if she is without make-up or jewels. A body without grace, a clumsy mind, a boor—these are "simple"; while he who presents himself well, who is aware of himself in all realms, is never called simple. Simplicity is a supreme refinement, a supreme choice, a supreme distinction. It is a result, a consequence—a rejection of the cliché for the expression that is art. It is a proof of awareness, it is an inner ease. Simplicity means to be concerned with what one is and what one hopes to become. It is a proof of the soul's beginning.

In 1914 Margaret Anderson had founded the *Little Review*, a revolutionary magazine of the arts "making no compromise with the public taste." It was the most interesting art publication in America and was the first to print, in serial form, the masterpiece which changed the trend of contemporary English literature— James Joyce's "Ulysses."

I had imagined that the young generation of American artists were still at the "intellectual" stage and that they would not interest me. I was mistaken. They were young but not unripe; emotional, romantic of temperament but not of mind; eager and dedicated. With Margaret and her collaborator, Jane Heap, I began to participate in the absorbing art life of New York.

But the value of these new friendships was not in the realm of art, it was rather in the life of ideas to which Margaret and Jane were so invincibly dedicated. For the first time in many years—

ever since the disintegration of the great motives upon which
Maeterlinck and I had built our existence—I found myself again
living for the life of the mind. Margaret, Jane and I began to talk,
with Monique as interpreter. Within a month Margaret could
manage a rudimentary French in which, strangely enough, she
could convey only important ideas, and our talk was that infinite
talk of infinite things which alone gives life vitality. This, at last,
was my justification for coming to a new world; this was what
I had tried to invoke, for my brother, when I cried out that my
life was not finished but only beginning; this was the resumption
and development of my aspirations, of my faith in that "impulse
to being" which is the raison d'être of living.

In all our talk we were not surprised to discover in each other
an identical striving and research; no barrier of geography, na-
tionality, generation or language divided us, and we were able to
produce a miracle of communication on an eternal subject matter—that of man's struggle to understand something of the mys-
teries within himself and the universe.

One night we went to hear a lecture on Ouspensky and his
"Tertium Organum." Although I did not know it then, this event
was to mark all my future. It was on that night that I heard for
the first time the ideas of a man called Gurdjieff. He had lived
for many years in the monasteries of Tibet, he had lately been
teaching in Russia, Germany, England and France, and was soon
coming to America. The transcendent ideas of this man fell like
the rays of a summer sun on my winter field, and I knew that at
last I had found a direction for my future.

In my wanderings about New York I had discovered, in West
Seventy-third Street, the narrow white tower of the Nobleton
Hotel and had often wished I could live there. When we found
that we could rent two small rooms at a very modest price on the
fifteenth floor, with a fire-escape leading to a roof which would
be ours alone, we left the Commodore and went to live in the

tower as if in an observatory. Our piano was too large for the elevator and had to be dismembered like a chicken. Margaret and Allen brought gifts collected by their friends . . . and flowers and flowers.

The very first night we climbed the fire-escape, clinging to the railing. Every step, made of narrow iron bars, traced a noteless staff of music in space. The activity that belonged to the sky was reversed and, by the million, stars appeared on the earth. I loved being there, suspended in space, as in the basket of a balloon.

Notes from a Diary

April. Sometimes curiosity keeps me on my tower until dawn, looking down on the fantastic aspects of the city. A certain vapor is in the air—a young fresh smell. It comes from the sea, it is the smell of a New York morning. I watch again and again the belated awakening of the city as it comes to life at eight-thirty.

How different from the gradual awakening of Paris—at four o'clock a few footsteps, at five the big trucks, at six the whole city in vibration, at six-thirty the full momentum of the day.

I feel that I love this city. It is logical, like a spinal column. Buildings in the sky—why not? There is always room above, and the sap of the race pushes strongly upward.

The rhythm of New York is that of a fair. Roller coasters rush me up into the sky, hurl me down again, and at the bottom of the abyss I rebound in the air. In no country, in no milieu of Europe, is such a life imaginable. Is it the influence of the air, so volatile, so electrified? Nothing is heavy and nothing is serious. Americans do not think in the same way as we do: they think of how to become more free, they never hesitate or retrace their steps, they are never resigned to anything. They are sustained, buoyed up, pushed forward.

Is it charm, intelligence, or kindness that I love most in the American character? I often analyze my contentment at being among these people. What I love is their way of living with temperament. In my country it is different—temperament only serves work or action, like a mechanism. In America it is in evidence everywhere, it is the daily bread, the indispensable. Even practical people have temperament here. I have seen businessmen effervesce, become intoxicated with life like artists. I watch the way two American men greet each other—they are two children, two minds colliding gaily, like racket and ball.

From the point of view of traditional European hypocrisy, the American character is as extraordinary as the country itself. I was astounded the first time I saw Margaret open the door to a caller and say to her simply, "I'm sorry, but I'm not at home today." I found this device both comic and commendable. In this country one breathes in freedom with the air of the race—a feminine air, of an exciting honesty.

When a Frenchwoman receives a compliment she murmurs a protest; an American replies with an energetic "Thank you." She cannot doubt a truth that is agreeable because disagreeable truths are spoken so frankly. To be outspoken is an innate American virtue, found especially in the women, since timidity silences nearly all the men—at least in the presence of a European woman.

End of April. Always the struggle, always the vicious circle from which I cannot escape. I don't recognize myself in all this chaos, but I am not troubled by it.

Why does Elizabeth Marbury, who knows the French spirit, advise me to abandon the struggle with the *Sunday Ameri-*

can? Is she so sure of my defeat? Even so, I have answered that I will fight just the same. She said, "Luck is the art of seizing fortune as it passes." Yes, but to do that one has to be attentive to outside things, and they are the things I do not understand. We don't get on well together.

To the artist, any material tragedy is like an iron cage. His real life slips out between the bars.

I have seen the house of Edgar Allen Poe—so touching. An adorable old cottage in a garden, a little corner of peace and poetry respected among the modern buildings that rise all around it. An old woman showed us the little rooms. On a high mantelpiece in the dining room was a stuffed blackbird. "It was his raven," she said.

I have been ill. Through the mists of fever I saw Margaret and Monique—two faces, one anguish. In brief moments of lucidity I had a vision of what life would be like with these two cherished friends, so different, and yet so alike in the love they accord me. I said nothing, however, being accustomed to allow great things to shape themselves, according to the laws that are within them. Between us a unity has been established which will give us an adorable and spacious existence.

Going to the summit of our tower was like going to a mountain retreat; at dawn there was a freshness like a wind from a lake. When I was well again I descended from these heights each day to go to Wall Street, in search of a new lawyer.

Although it was only May, a ceiling of fire hung low over the streets. The sun's rays machine-gunned pedestrians; people fell dead. In such heat my costume was a source of curiosity and solicitude. Our five hundred dollars was exhausted and I hadn't been able to buy any summer clothes. I wore a long cape to hide my dark winter dress, and a big white felt hat undulated heavily on my head. As it couldn't withstand another cleaning, Monique had thought of powdering it with flour. At the slightest breeze a powdery cloud floated down around me. Wherever I went everyone was determined to relieve me of my cape and I had to insist that I was not too warm. How kind everyone was in those New York offices! A chain of smiles accompanied me from door to door. I knew that each lawyer would put my dossier in a drawer where it would suffer the fate of problems better left unsolved, yet after each interview I walked forth with a new courage, comforted by friendly words. I took them all home to Monique who was always waiting for me anxiously. When was she not anxious?—this gentle friend who shared my troubles with such quietness. Those who know her call her Saint Monique. But there is nothing rigorous or petty in her saintliness. She is a character met only in books with colored illustrations, a being whose words and steps make no sound, and who always offers to agree with me.

I went through the business-filled days automatically, my thoughts always concentrated on the night I would spend on my tower. Those were sovereign nights in spite of the exiled stars. I contrasted them with other, so different, nights when the skies of France outlined the arches of the cloister I loved; or extended, bare, black and infinite, over the fields.

Sometimes as the sun rose I watched skyscrapers emerge slowly from the mist, like a flotilla of icebergs. Standing there, I could laugh a little at my futile war with a newspaper—the struggle of an ant with a giant straw. In spite of it, in spite of everything, I felt essentially free. I knew that a new life, made of what I had lived, learned and longed for, was forming within me. I knew that when this senseless adventure was ended I would be ready for that life in which the false reality extolled by the world would disappear before a true reality. This would not come to pass all at once, but each month, each year, would bring me closer to the essential question: the reason for my existence.

Notes from a Diary

May 16. I have three reasons for not leaving America: I must stay for my projects; I must stay for my new life; and I must stay in order not to go back into darkness.

The thoughts of my present life run through my head like a refrain. I came here to live a different life from the one I lived in France, a life of the work I love, a life in which I could watch the past fading away and the future emerging; but now I struggle only to keep alive. Yet who knows whether struggle is not a way to wisdom, who knows whether I am not perhaps fortunate to live through so many misfortunes for the sake of my own truth. The important thing is to feel one's existence, and hunger makes me feel my existence day and night.

We conceal our worst difficulties from Margaret—she herself hasn't enough to eat. Although people often help her magazine with donations, she has nothing for herself. Allen also lives without money. They are both courage-machines.

Sometimes we have moments of relaxation. When artists receive even a little money they share it and celebrate. We assemble around a table where a single flower reigns, little gifts are exchanged which are touching in their simplicity always wrapped with great forethought, for the real present is the surprise of its presentation.

I begin to understand the nature of what I experience continually in this country—generosity and its special psychology. It doesn't consist merely of admiration for and lionization of the artist. It is deeper—it is organic. Americans have so genuine a need to be generous that the gratitude one feels toward them becomes reciprocal—they almost thank the person who allows them to exercise their generosity. They have a pre-generosity that doesn't consider whether or not it is deserved. In other races there is something umbilical between the giver and the gift.

It doesn't displease me to be completely poor. What angers me is that the need to eat not only drains my vitality but attacks my mind, my imagination. It becomes a mental obsession. I live all this in the strange half-sleep that is the result of hunger, I have become accustomed to that heaviness at the back of the neck, that pain over the eyes, the strain of muscles holding up a head suddenly too heavy.

Just as I was beginning to think that these dark days would end, Véral, embarrassed and apologetic, came to ask me to release him from our contract. He had decided to abandon all his great projects and leave for Europe. "I am sorry," he said, "but events are stronger than I am." What was not stronger than he? I consented at once and we formally tore up the paper which would have bound me to him for four more years. In spite of this he dared to say as he left, "I am certain that you will have the success you deserve, and while I am away I count on you to send me my thirty per cent on whatever you make." Thus ended our burlesque partnership, and when the door closed behind him I was filled with a sense of freedom.

Later in the day there was more good news. Margaret was to be alone for the summer and invited Monique and me to live in her apartment. Although it meant exchanging a tower for a street, I was overjoyed at the thought of sharing the inspired daily life of the *Little Review*.

Monique preceded us to the apartment in Eighth Street and had just time, before our arrival, to tack up on the wall as a greeting one of my favorite axioms: Goethe's "Tout est bien, il suffit d'être maître de soi." We agreed, helpless with laughter.

As I watched Margaret day by day in Eighth Street, I often thought of Montaigne's words: "An absolute perfection, resembling divinity—to know how to enjoy one's own being."

Margaret is more instantaneous than other people. For her there is no journey to be made from seeing to speaking or acting. She "arrives" immediately, as if all the minutes of her life had served as an exercise in the promptness and accuracy of her reflexes.

I know of no one more free, more frank, more exposed and at the same time more natively mysterious. She who is so civilized has retained certain primitive reactions. She has only active gestures. She doesn't wander about a room, she walks into it and chooses her place; she doesn't fall into a chair, she sits down; she doesn't chatter, she talks. When she talks about the weather it is only to praise it—rain or sunshine, heat or cold, are greeted with equal enchantment. She refuses to bother about her health. Never a coat over her arm, always both hands free. To carry an object is a crime.

Her apartment is like a still-life which cannot move from its imaginary frame. She has a tape-measure in her eye. Her own room is like a chord of music, each object a note that plays its part. Close to her bed are her mules, standing side by side like two steeds, harnessed and ready to go.

Margaret paints life as one paints a canvas. She not only arranges the apartment, she prepares the days. Each one must fit into the week like an object in its case. When all is in order, she is one with her surroundings. From her window, even the branches of the trees in the garden look as if they had passed through her hands to decorate the sky.

When I first met her she possessed only one suit, a thousand times mended and cleaned, like her gloves and stockings. In any kind of weather she did her errands on foot, in patent leather pumps, but, she always looked as if she had just stepped out of a limousine. I loved her airy walk, her light vibrations; I loved her

hard perseverance, her intransigent mind; and I loved the inner
beatitude which always adorned her beauty. Her spirit is both eager and essentially serious; suffering frightens her, but she doesn't
know what it is to complain. She is cowardly and brave at the
same time, and without effort she always seems happy even when
she is sad.

My latest lawyer had finally come to an agreement with the
Sunday American. I would consent to the publication, in order
to reimburse the money I had received in advance, but on two
conditions: that Margaret should correct certain vulgarities in
the translation and that "no injurious epithet, no hurtful word,
would be attached to the name of Maeterlinck." When Margaret
corrected the proofs she left my text intact.

After a year of battles I seemed to have emerged victorious.
On the day before the publication, happy and unsuspecting, I
decided to go to the offices of the *Sunday American* and bring
home the first copies to come off the press.

As I approached the entrance of the newspaper building I noticed long strips of red paper lying in the street. Men were tossing bundles of posters into trucks and driving off with them. At
the entrance door I saw posters pasted on the walls—two enormous scarlet hearts pierced by a black arrow. Red ink like spat-
tered blood was spread over two names—Maeterlinck's name
and mine. Above them was the title of my memoirs, and below
in flaming letters was printed: "Twenty Years of Love without
Marriage." My lawyer had neglected to supervise the publicity . . .

Unable to move, I stood in the street a long time, suffocated by
the sight before my eyes. This, then, was the result of my victory. I
imagined the red tide rushing everywhere, through all the streets
of the city—our unearthly love transported from the abbey of
St. Wandrille to the gutters of New York. I clenched my hands
together, as if they could hold back the tide.

CHAPTER THREE
VICTORY IN DEFEAT

AFTER all that I had lived through in New York I needed trees, air, grass—all the health of the earth to regain my own.

We had been told of houses to rent in Bernardsville, New Jersey, for the end of the summer. Margaret borrowed our railroad fare and we set out to inspect them. A real estate agent was waiting for us, but he showed us only great estates, renting for hundreds of dollars a month. Finally he turned his car into a long avenue of cypress trees. At the far end was a large grey house, gay and rambling, with a rose garden, an old park and wooded hills that blended with the sky. "One hundred and fifty dollars a month," said the agent, "but it's not much of a place—there are only four servants' rooms."

The next day Dodd Mead advanced me a hundred dollars and a pawnshop furnished the remainder of the first month's rent. We were again penniless when we moved into the house in Bernardsville, but as we entered the sun was shining on the Victory of Samothrace in the hall and we hailed it as a good omen. The principal grocery store in the village telephoned for our patronage and Allen gave a colossal order. Immediately everything in the town was at our disposal, including a Steinway piano.

The first evening in Bernardsville we gathered on the main terrace. Vistas had been cut in the woods around the estate to make horizons and I could see distant blue hills which lay like smoke across the valley, with a rising red moon at the end of the cypress avenue. The silhouette of the trees, reaching into the distance, seemed to touch the moon.

Allen had heard of a young composer, George Antheil, the favorite pupil of Ernest Bloch. We invited him to spend a day with us and he answered, "I will come with pleasure since you are interested in modern musics." His plural intrigued us.

An astonishing young person arrived, short, square-shoul-dered and with the spotty complexion of adolescence. But he car-ried within him that silent assurance which is the mark of a pre-cocious self-awareness. The disproportion of his body and head, the fixed intense expression of his eyes, his fierce preoccupation with his own thought gave me an impression of genius.

He shook hands with each of us without curiosity, as if he had left us the day before. Then, seeing the piano across the room, he rushed at it. For two long hours we listened to him, mesmerized. In his music was his explanation and his reason for being. When he played his face changed completely, he was no longer red and ugly; an even pallor spread over his features and they became al-most classic. Later he told us the tragedy of his existence—the tragedy of those who live in a family which has either finished living or has never lived at all. He said with simplicity that when he received our letter he told his parents he was coming to live with us. He had brought all his possessions in a cardboard suit-case—manuscripts, music paper, pencils, India ink and rulers. In the midst of these treasures were one shirt and two pairs of socks, since he had neither pajamas nor bathrobe he accepted one of our bathrobes and a pair of sandals.

He worked almost all day and half the night, stopping only when fatigue or sleep overwhelmed him. He never seemed to eat. This upset us until Allen discovered that a sack of green apples was almost empty and cans of baked beans were missing from the pantry. Evidently George was simplifying his life and we no longer worried about his immateriality. But we suffered under his manner of composing. He would choose a theme of five or six notes and repeat it insatiably for hours on end. He seemed to hypnotize himself with certain vibrations; then he would rush to his room and write until the following morning.

Each of us worked alone during the day, not meeting (except for lunch) until tea-time. We dined at nine and then our great hours began. I sang Mélisande with Allen, whose fluid voice created a Pelléas that surpassed any I ever heard in a theatre. George played his "Ballet Mécanique" which had the honor of being hissed in Paris three years later. Allen, who lived more at the piano than he did in life, played Debussy and Ravel, Chopin, Schumann, Bach, and his piano transcription of Scriabin's "Poème de l'Extase." Margaret listened in her own lyrical manner. Sometimes, worn-out by vibrations, she rested her beautiful head on the window-sill, and, capped with moonlight, slumbered in a halo.

When I think of those rare moments, two memories outshine the others: an early dawn when Bach's deepest pages became for me almost a discovery; and a hot heavy night, filled with the life of flowers, which we dedicated to Strauss's "Rosenkavalier." I remember the adorable waltz as a pool of light where lovely dancers turned and turned, exhausted with dizziness and grace.

Two o'clock in the morning was supper time, and the hour of stories and laughter. Sometimes we had guests—a young poet, Mark Turbyfill, read his latest poem, "Conversation is in Heaven"; a young lawyer played a flute to satisfy his poetic dreams, scattering little sounds of rapture pitifully into the great night. Then Allen would intone a hymn of parting and we separated. In the rising dawn there remained only the soft and muffled cry of an owl.

The seasons pass quickly in America. The month of October had already given us a beautiful autumn, and we knew that winter would soon overtake us, for America is a country of sudden changes where nature moves quickly. The trees still held their colored leaves when the cold arrived one day with a thin, hard snow.

The tradespeople had by now ceased their attentions and we found ourselves beset by impossibilities—impossible to leave without paying our bills, impossible to live in New York without money, impossible to buy coal, impossible to stay on without heat. An inspiration was needed and it was Monique who supplied it by discovering a wood-burning stove in one of the cellars. Although the room was dark, a big electric light bulb hung over an iron-table and a ray of daylight entered from a row of casement windows. Through them we could see a rim of earth and a few tree-trunks. I guessed Monique's idea at once—why not live in this cellar while awaiting events? We would sleep upstairs in the cold and descend in the morning to a warm life around the wood stove.

We installed ourselves at once, carrying down chairs and a chaise-longue, rugs, writing-table, bookcase, firewood, some china and the last of our provisions—cereals and a few tins of food—which we hid behind a screen. We even found two men to carry down the piano. Allen placed candlesticks on the table, a flowered scarf around the light-bulb and some branches in a vase. The stove roared, the canary sang and we gaily drank the last of our Russian tea.

George left for Philadelphia, where he hoped to give recitals, and Margaret and Allen went to New York to see the concert managers for me. I was to remain in the country with Monique, connected with the outside world only by the telephone.

Weeks went by, unmarked by any event. I was happy in our cellar and I lived intensely in a strong inner world of silence. Our solitude was total. Snow protected the winter stillness, muting even the sounds of animal life which reached us but faintly; no birds, no bells, no movement but that of the soft snowflakes which seemed to die of their silent fall, yet hour by hour widened the white band at the windows. I watched them with upturned face, as I sat at the table reading or writing; and I waited without impatience for the sound of the telephone which would ring in the great empty house above us, to bring news of the outside world.

Every morning at nine o'clock I found Monique kneeling before the cellar stove in her brown dress, a shawl around her shoulders, her black braids arranged like two little curtains drawn back to show her face, radiating peace and goodness.

At this hour a little sunlight slipped down our walls. We missed seeing the sky and we would go out to look at it whenever the snow stopped falling, but it was always hidden in a frosty mist. Space had neither form nor color and we would return quickly to our cell. My day began. I knew it would be intact and that was enough to feel it within me like a flow of beatitude.

It was while watching the snow fall against the black frame of the window that, for the first time, I began to write poetry. As I sat enclosed within the four walls of grey stone, some lines in praise of green came from the end of my pencil, like a primary color all fresh from the palette, and I wrote a poem to spring. A new gift of feeling had come to me. A poem, for a poet, is not merely a literary impulsion but an urgent and veritable necessity. A poet lives, enclosed, in the silent events of his clamorous world. Poetry is the event which takes place between himself and language.

Early in December I sang at a private soirée in New York and thus was able to pay our debts and leave Bernardsville. In Washington Place, Greenwich Village, I discovered a studio apartment, in old Norman style, with a terrace surrounded by trees.

But again mishaps began to follow like a procession of caterpillars—if the chain is broken for a moment it forms again at once. A potential manager fractured his skull in an automobile accident; another went bankrupt; and a generous woman who wanted me to help her found a French Conservatory in New York suddenly died.

We just managed to live. Some new friends organized a series of subscription matinées and I sold some articles and drawings to a newspaper. In June Olga Samaroff Stokowski, the pianist, invited me to visit her in Bar Harbor and give a concert in the

Temple of Art, built on a hill overlooking the sea. Walter Damrosch, conductor of the New York Symphony, accompanied the classical part of the program, while Samaroff accompanied the Ravel, Milhaud, Poulenc and Stravinsky songs. This was one of the beautiful concerts of my life. The doors of the Temple were open and as I sang I looked out over bright lawns and black pines to the rhythms of the silent sea.

I met Leopold Stokowski and at once we began to talk of organizing a great manifestation of art. He suggested a grandiose setting for such a project—George Grey Barnard's gothic cloister on upper Riverside Drive, filled with treasures of the Middle Ages brought from France. We would begin with the choir music of Palestrina and I would sing rare pages of Bach, Gluck and Monteverdi, which Stokowski would orchestrate. The acoustics were perfect, an orchestra of forty musicians would be hidden in an upper gallery, and the proceeds would be given to French and Belgian orphans. In this presentation I would recapture something of the grandeur and unique beauty of the "Macbeth" and "Pelléas" productions in St. Wandrille. The prospect of such a debut in New York exceeded anything I had dreamed of.

When Stokowski went back to his country house near Philadelphia I went there to rehearse with him. He played his superb orchestrations on the piano, filling the studio with waves of sound. He himself interested me—his precision of movement, his sharp glance and accelerated rhythms, his childlike outbursts of enthusiasm.

Our matinée was fixed for the thirtieth of October. On the nineteenth, in a despairing telegram, Stokowski announced a catastrophe. His letter followed:

Dear Georgette Leblanc,
    The directors of the Philadelphia Orchestra will not consent to my giving a concert in New York without the full orchestra of a hundred and fifty musicians. They introduced this

rule into the statutes about two years ago, and I must confess
that I had completely forgotten it. Yesterday I insisted again
to the management. They are absolutely opposed to the idea
that the Orchestra play in New York beyond the series of its
established programs and with a reduced number of musicians. I feel that I should not attempt this matinée by gath-
ering together musicians I could find in New York. I know
that you understand the immense work I have done with my
orchestra for the past ten years, rehearsing every morning for
seven months of the year to obtain the quality of tone, flex-
ibility of rhythm and ensemble of phrasing which is my ideal.
To a certain degree I have attained all that; but in two or three
rehearsals it would be impossible for me even to approach the
results which took me so many years to achieve here. My only
thought in arranging this matinée was to collaborate with you
in a manifestation of art of the highest quality. I cannot forgive myself for having forgotten the practical side. I am truly
sorry.

Leopold Stokowski.

There was nothing to do but destroy the programs and posters,
and return to subscribers the $2,000 already received from the
advance sale of tickets.

I gave a new series of subscription concerts, made three hundred dollars a matinée and many enthusiastic new friends. I see
their faces still, I remember what each one did for me, but there
were so many of them that I no longer know their names. I am
grateful to them as one is grateful to nature or to a tree that one
cherishes, without loving separately each of its leaves.

The Saviors

Each morning for a week Monique had noticed a large dark
woman standing beneath our windows. One day she stopped

Monique in the street and gave her an article she had written about me in a Brooklyn newspaper, but which she had been too shy to send. It was signed "J. Barelli" and in the margin the author had added: "She who passes religiously before your door." Monique was sympathetic to such piety. Madame Barelli said that her admiration for me dated from a recent concert in which I had sung some modern French songs. But it was not the modern that had most captivated her and her husband—it was a famous page of Reynaldo Hahn's that I had sung as an encore. "Never, never, signora," she said, "have I heard 'Infidélité' sung as by Georgette Leblanc."

Monique brought her in to see me. She told me that she and her husband were in the concert business and had been eagerly waiting to hear me sing again. In her extreme ardor she could scarcely believe that I had no future engagements, that I was not besieged by managers.

The next day Madame Barelli and her husband came together to Washington Place. They stood before me, their strongly Italianized faces glowing with emotion. She was enormous and resembled a church bell with a Roman profile at the top. The husband, very thin, feverishly agitated, always half hidden in his wife's great bulk, made me think of the clapper of the bell. She was the music critic of an Italian newspaper in Brooklyn, where they lived; he claimed long experience in the concert field. They had come to implore me to let them be my managers; they were ready to back me with their life savings and assured me that my success would be overwhelming, given the opportunity of a concert in Town Hall under their auspices. I accepted their offer, convinced that such enthusiasm could only lead to great things.

I felt less certain of my judgment in the days that followed. After the Town Hall had been engaged, the Barellis began to reveal extraordinary ideas of management: they refused to advertise the concert in the usual way, hinting that they had original methods of their own. As the weeks went by, these mysterious methods worried us more and more, but Barelli was beyond all control and would only repeat like a magician, "You will see, watch closely. Wait for my surprise."

Three days before the concert Barelli telephoned, that his surprise was ready—we were to go and see it at the corner of Broadway and Forty-second Street. He was waiting for us and pointed at the sky. There, above the signs that advertised chewing-gums, soaps, vacuum cleaners and floor polish, I saw a poster-portrait of myself, enormous in reality but from the street a miniature. The boundless enthusiasm of the Barellis had exalted me toward the infinite, convinced that such an ascension into the ether, so saintly a place among the stars, would, be irresistible to the public. Allen tried to explain that New York concert managers never used the heavens for musical advertisements, nor did concert-goers look for them there. But Barelli, drunk with importance, was incapable of listening. He could only stare at the sky, unaware that the success of the concert, together with his money, had disappeared into the clouds.

On the night of the concert, at the entrance to the Town Hall, the Barellis stationed themselves on either side of the box-office. In a loud voice he proclaimed to the public that he was about to impose a new law in the concert world: none of the usual free tickets would be available and even the critics could not enter without paying for their seats. In approval Madame Barelli thumped the floor with her umbrella, occasionally shouting the incredible words, "No dead heads for Georgette Leblanc." In defiance, one of the critics managed to slip into the hall—Barelli pounced upon him, took him by the collar and threw him out. Thereupon most of my potential audience left in disgust, though many of the critics paid for their tickets and remained.

Facing an almost empty house, I invited the scattered few into the front rows and sang to them. (Incidentally, the reviews in the next morning's papers were most kind.)

Washington Square South

For the past year my friends had watched the rise and fall of my fortunes like the line of a temperature chart. They had done their best to help me and now they were tired; they thought I should return to France. I understood their discouragement, but *I* was not tired. Already I had a new plan.

Margaret and I began to search Greenwich Village for a place where I could give small concerts—a studio, a basement, a vacant shop. We found something better—the ground floor of an old house, destined for demolition, at forty-seven Washington Square South.

We entered a hall, pushed open a door and stood spellbound, for at the end of the long room we saw a stage ... Beyond were two bedrooms, a studio, kitchen, bath. Everything was falling apart—ceilings were cracked, radiators broken, electric wires torn out. Each sign of disaster made my hopes rise—who but myself would want to rent such a place? The astonished landlord let us have it for thirty dollars a month.

As soon as we moved to Washington Square a deluge of gifts arrived from the friends who, having advised me to give up hope, were now sure of my success. They sent furniture, rugs, lamps and a blue velvet curtain which we hung across the stage. Allen arranged the footlights and Margaret hypnotized the Mason and Hamlin Company into lending us a grand piano.

We sent out invitations for a tea and so many people accepted that my small theatre was filled. I made a little speech from the stage, saying that I was going to give a concert in this room every night, that I had prepared ten programs for ten consecutive weeks, and that I would continue to sing here until a backer or manager appeared. After my speech everyone bought subscription tickets from Monique who sat beaming at a little table by the door.

I opened my theatre that same week. Each day there were telephone calls for seats and nearly every evening people were turned away, owing to lack of space. The concerts began at nine and were supposed to finish at eleven, but rarely did the audience let me stop before midnight. Several times I sang until two in the morning.

Thus I launched myself in immense New York, without either money or a manager.

I have given hundreds of concerts in my life, but the formal concert with its ceremonial pace is a torture to me. To cut one's emotion into a thousand crumbs, bow after each crumb, leave the stage, come on again, bow again, throw a discreet glance toward the accompanist to signal "begin," look serene while one's arteries beat furiously; then if there is a moment of internal distraction, the slightest disruption of "the state," all is lost. The formal concert, to me, is anti-natural and its form has always disturbed me even when I am in the audience. In the old days when the singer appeared on the platform, bust extended, white gloves clenched around her sheet of music, oval mouth sending out the sound to right and left like an automatic distributor, I always wanted to flee.

I enjoy giving concerts when I can create an atmosphere that is simple and vital. I love to bring the public into close relation to my thought, in an intimacy without ornament or vanity. This was possible on my little stage in Washington Square, where I often spoke as much as I sang. Sometimes I sat near the edge of the stage and began the evening by talking of my songs and their composers. In this way I could be my real self—I hate everything that does not stem from reality. The night Sarah Bernhardt died I did not sing at all, I could only talk of her—of her courageous life and her magical art. The audience asked torrents of questions and although our evening was without song, the room was filled with the music of her memory.

On the night of the sixty-third concert Monique came running backstage in a flurry of excitement to tell me that a group of eight people had come to hear me for the third time. Peeping through the curtain, I found them at once. They were all in evening dress—three white-haired men and a woman with beautiful jewels, accompanied by four younger people. When the concert was over they sent me their cards and asked if they might stay and talk with me. Monique brought them into the studio and we all sat down around the fire. One of the men, Mr. D., began by saying, in French, that an artist like myself should be heard all over America; and that, if I would accept their help, they would like to make this possible.

How brightly the details of that hour still live in me—the blue sofa on which I sat, the long shadows stretching on the walls, the leaping flames that illumined with a floating light those faces I had never seen until tonight. These sympathetic strangers were offering me the life and work I so longed for. While they outlined their plans for me my mind whirled like a merry-go-round. I kept repeating to myself, "It's a fairy-tale, how can they know everything I desire? Is this really happening to me?" I listened as in a trance while they planned how they would organize an art corporation which would feature all my talents—singing, acting, writing, and lecturing. These people considered me a business and I was almost dead of happiness. I had always dreamed of being exploited like an object—"Will you do this or that, and on what date?"; to be free of all business talk; to have just enough to live on, leaving the rest of the profits to the company, but in heaven's name not to participate in the life of the box-office, when I said good night to them I felt something of the awe one always feels when the impossible has been made to happen because of one's indomitable belief in it.

During the next week we discussed plans almost daily. After everything had been settled, Mr. D. came to Washington Square to say that it would be simpler if he alone assumed the direction of the corporation, suggesting that I be president, Margaret vice-president, and he himself business manager and general director. I accepted and the next day we signed the formal papers.

The Tragedy of the Excessive

I had already experienced American generosity, but now I was to know super-generosity. I had wanted necessities, now I was surfeited with luxuries. A chauffeur was always stationed at the door and I was submerged with prima donna gifts. Of all these the only offerings I really enjoyed were the enormous boxes of bonbons and the great baskets of hothouse fruits from which Monique made that American ambrosia—grape juice filled with peaches, oranges, grapefruit, pineapples, cherries and bananas, sparkling through a crystal pitcher like a jeweler's window.

When an office was rented in my name in one of the tallest buildings in the city, my state bordered on ecstasy. This high heaven consisted of two rooms—one for me and one for my personal manager, Louise Davidson, with her secretary. Typewriters stood ready for action under their oilcloth covers, and on the shelves were stacks of stationery engraved with the words, "Art Direction Georgette Leblanc, Inc." With such an organization I would be able to help other artists arriving in America as I had, with nothing but dreams. This idea still shines in my memory as the gold letters of my name shone on that door on the twenty-third floor of the Fisk Building.

The fairy-tale continued through the spring and I never suspected that it might come to an end. But unfortunately I have never lived wisely in relation to great happiness—I consume it with all my strength. Instead of foreseeing possible pitfalls in this unprecedented utopia, I treated it as if it were inexhaustible. Blissful and imprudent, I decided to go to Paris and bring back to America all the interesting new music of the modern French composers. During my absence a coast-to-coast concert tour would be prepared for the autumn, Mr. D. having decided that it would be easier to launch me as an arrival from the French capital than as an artist who had been stranded in New York for two years. Margaret, Monique and I sailed for France at the end of May.

In Paris, at the suggestion of my corporation, I rented an apartment in a beautiful old house in a beautiful old garden in rue Vaneau. Then from New York I began to receive letters from the head of the corporation, practical, full of business advice. Gradually their tone changed and they became personal. I was urged to buy a château, jewels, furs. I could only pretend not to understand, confident that my seeming blindness would be enough to prevent the customary—and classic—debacle. That confidence was abruptly shattered by a letter—an all-too-human letter, as desolating as it was precise.

I did not hesitate a second . . . The fairy-tale had lasted four months.

I returned immediately to New York to salvage what I could of the situation. My office in the Fisk Building was closed and the gold letters on the door no longer shone. The corporation had been dissolved, but a sum of money had been set aside to meet the expenses of the coast-to-coast concert tour. Although I knew the perils of such an undertaking, I started out with victorious conviction.*

The tour was all I had hoped for—indeed I can almost call it a miracle, since I owed no money at the end. My greatest re-

---

* Margaret Caroline Anderson, 1972: The reality was this: A protégé who meant to marry Mr. D'Aoust for his money accused Georgette of being an adventuress who was planning to marry him for his money, and promptly did this herself. . . . The grotesque scandal left Georgette without protest. She returned a checkbook with thousands of dollars in blank checks, withdrew from the corporation, and let things run their course. We talked very little of the melodrama, but three years later Georgette wrote in her diary: "It is obvious that he hurt me so profoundly that all my strength faltered during the past three years. Finally this drama is over, and I can live again."

ward from it was the appreciation I found everywhere, even in the smaller cities, for the exquisite music of France.

Back in New York, many of my friends insisted that I should take legal action against my corporation. No, a thousand times no. There are beautiful seasons in human lives; one must learn that they pass quickly. I have nothing but infinite gratitude toward those people who wanted to give me what they judged to be more than that which I wanted.

And, besides, my attention was already elsewhere. I have spoken of an event which was to change the course of my life. It now took place. The man named Gurdjieff, whose "unknown doctrine" had so impressed me a year before at the Ouspensky lecture, gave his first talk in America. As I listened to him speak of God, the universe and man, I realized that for the first time I had come upon a cosmology that gave promise of not ending in an impasse.

I resolved that nothing would prevent me from hearing more of this man's vast knowledge. My corporation had guaranteed our return passage to Europe and I began to put my affairs in order. A few months later, when Gurdjieff announced his return to France, we were ready to follow.

CHAPTER FOUR
THE FLOWERING OF A FIELD

A ND so it was that in June, 1924, Margaret, Jane, Monique and I went to stay at the Château du Prieuré in Fontaine-bleau-Avon, for it was there that Gurdjieff lived and received people who sought him out from all over the world.

My impression of Gurdjieff was that he resided on the earth as on a planet too limited for his own needs and function. Where did he manifest his real existence? In his teaching, in his writings, not at all in ordinary social life which he seemed to regard as a joke and manipulated with resignation or impatience.

I was not at all astonished that he was little known, that he was not surrounded by thousands of followers. Neither money nor influence could open the doors of the Prieuré—Gurdjieff created all possible obstacles to discourage any idlers who might push their way into a world where they did not belong.

I have never been able to acclimatize myself to esoteric cults and doctrines with their vague followers—instinctively I turn away. On the contrary, the sharp climate of Gurdjieff's menta-tion held me. It was a difficult climate; to live in it one had to possess an invincible need.

To know something of the stature of the man one had to lis-ten to the reading of his manuscript—an enormous work in nine parts. My silent listening disappointed many in the audience who expected some audible sign of my interest; but I was entirely pre-occupied in the process of *absorbing*, like a plant that has waited for water all its life.

"I cannot develop you," Gurdjieff told us, "I can create condi-tions in which you can develop yourselves."

Those conditions were hard, yet my greatest distress was not to have known earlier this hard instruction. In the beginning it seemed heartbreaking to approach such truths at last and to have

44

so few years left to give to them. But soon the fact that I was working within myself, with an unawakened part of my nature, supplied me with a new strange energy. From now on I would know how to use the time remaining to me—I pictured myself as a honeycomb with each cell waiting to be filled.

I followed avidly the daily monastic life of the Prieuré—the conversations, the readings, the communal work in the gardens. Each day I tried to foresee the stages through which I would pass and I laughed at myself, at this poor human being who dared to say: "I want 'to be', I dedicate my life to this end." It was like saying "I shall work to fly like a bird." A scale ran from tadpole to bird, and I did not know the number of notes. I knew only that each note led to the next and that nothing in the world—book, word or prophesy—would help me to know in advance what the next one would be. It would depend essentially on my organism.

What astonished me was not to understand a little but to see that some people—newcomers to the Prieuré—did not understand at all. I sometimes had flashes of "consciousness" so strong that a heat invaded me. Every hour I became aware of a "soul" I had not nurtured.

Two stories for each individual...himself and his shadow (that is, his "soul"). His appearance comes and goes with a name, a situation; his shadow—a reality which exists only by virtue of light—awaits its hour and makes its appearance only at the end. I saw myself, like all human beings, as a repetition-machine; and I had always aspired to a different state. Too long now I had rested in that illusory "I" that is like a Chinese figure of porcelain whose head nods "yes" perpetually to all our blindness's, perpetually approves all our acts. Now I wanted to finish with all that old automatic life, so pleasant but so null—human life which leads to nothing unless it leads to everything. I began to work to change, and I felt as if I were being torn from my roots. Why should I cling so hard to that which I no longer clung to, which I had never really clung to? Did I underestimate the power of the bonds which attached me to . . . nothing? Yes. I had thought myself different from my parents because I had lived my life differently. But what essential difference is there in that? It is only the menu of days, like the menu of meals.

I am always asked, in respect of this cosmogony which has now held my attention for so many years, "Is your source the same as Katherine Mansfield's?" I answer, "Yes, in fact; no, in essence."

In her journal, Katherine Mansfield wrote of the last months of her life at the Prieuré. It is not known that Gurdjieff had admitted her to his Institute with a reservation, that it was too late to help her physically, but possible to help her in other ways.

It is of these "other ways" that her journal and letters record less than she was able to express in her conversations with Orage* at the Prieuré. The greatness of Katherine was her sincerity. She was not pious, yet she felt the need of a redemption, of a system of "purity," she wanted a spiritual life stripped of the clichés of religion. This spirituality of which she had such a magnificent need can be had without recourse to Gurdjieff—it already exists in the best of religion. It can be had without great effort. Gurdjieff offers much more. He is not consoling; he is better than that. What he offers is hard, like the teaching of Jesus—if one gets to its source. There is no Truth that is obliging. I think that the first requisite for an approach to Gurdjieff is a condition of health; one must be able to withstand the first shocks. There is, to begin with, the inconceivable torment of feeling oneself like earth that is being ploughed up. All at once our forces are solicited for an unknown labor. It is impossible. The more one sees and understands the more one thinks: "I cannot." But is it our forces that are solicited? No. It is a question of forces that we have never

---

* A. R. Orage. One-time editor of the English New Age and known to many in America as the precursor and interpreter of Gurdjieff in New York in the twenties and thirties.

used, that we are ignorant of . . . new energies awakened by a new need, towards a new goal.

This awakening was what Katherine experienced with Gurdjieff's teaching at the Prieuré.

Although at the Prieuré I experienced a happiness beyond any I had ever known, I also fell from despair to despair. My anxiety was total, I lived the meaning of the word "distressed." At each instant I touched the depths of my distress—a vague distress in which I did not entirely participate. Even when a new flash of understanding came to me I felt more lost than ever. The essential that I was seeking remained hidden from my sight. My only hope of finding it lay in my capacity for effort.

"But why do you want this knowledge?" my old friends asked. Strange question. No one asks, "Why do you want happiness?" To me knowledge—or rather, understanding—is a perfect synonym for happiness. Others said, "Never look inside yourself, it is fatal"; or, "What can one do with one's life when one has lost all illusions?" I answered, "That's as if a farmer said, "All the weeds in my fields have been pulled up, what can I do with the ground now?"

Years and years ago I used to think: "Our natures should be ploughed up as the ground is ploughed." But where was the plough, and who would guide it? Alone we could do nothing. The plough and the planter were as necessary as the seed.

Gurdjieff's "method" indicated the instrument and the guide. They were ready and waiting; it was for me to be ready and willing. Wish, need, effort—it was with these requirements that one approached that "other life" with its special efforts, its new laws, its different evolution which tended to change even the chemistry of one's organism. It was to be a difficult life. At the Prieuré I watched certain people stop half-way, renounce or branch off, become enemies and enroll themselves in some promising system which guaranteed paradise at the end of their days. Sometimes they returned to religion and declared themselves "touched by grace"—a grace which usually corresponded to their most material needs and in which they installed themselves comfortably, with all their luggage, as if for a voyage. They took a one-way ticket to paradise, but I noticed that more often than not they changed it for a round-trip.

What an error it is to believe that suffering alone is enough for self-development. If it were, our planet would already be covered with saints and angels. Suffering kills some people; others are deformed by it; some become mad; only a few improve or progress. One must have more knowledge to benefit by suffering.

All my life I had instinctively been a believer, but I could not accept the God proposed by religion . . . a God conceived merely as a refuge or a hope, when He should be the divine progression of the soul which contains Him. But every human being is the mirror of the God he conceives, and most are pocket-mirrors.

During all my first months at the Prieuré my ground was being ploughed. For a long time I thought I had recognized my nothingness; for a long time I thought I had known my vanity. Now I saw that this judgment was still a kind of vanity. So I watched myself, I began to know myself a little.

CHAPTER FIVE
A LIGHTHOUSE AND A HUNTING LODGE

FOR two years we lived at intervals at the Prieuré. From then until 1935 we encountered Gurdjieff more rarely but we continued to live, as far as we could, according to his principles, incorporating his doctrine more and more deeply.

To solve the problem of material living we searched everywhere for a background of peace where we could work quietly and alone, finding it at last in an old Normandy village called Tancarville. We were living in the château and strolling one morning on a white road beside the Seine, we looked up to the top of a cliff and saw a turret, like a great tulip emerging from the woods on a grey sky. It was the belvedere of an abandoned lighthouse, suspended between heaven and earth. The peasants told us it had not been used for many years, that no one could live in it "on account of the boredom," that it couldn't even be approached because brambles had overgrown the path. Nevertheless we scaled the heights, rented it for fifty francs a month and installed ourselves as in the stratosphere. Every year, for thirteen years, at the green season, it has offered us its divine expanse of sky, fields and river.

Living in it, one fancies one's self travelling. Its beauty is transfigured at every moment of the day and night. Beacon lights pass softly across the water at evening, the silence is broken only by the metallic cry of gulls or the singsong murmur of night birds. The fog bell has a voice of transition and departure—clear with good weather, sad and breathless when the mist envelopes us. Here everything is excessive—the cold, the sun, the luxury of the stars. On nights of tempest one is shipwrecked and the dawn that returns to earth comes like a benediction.

For the winters, near Paris, I found something else—the Château de la Muette, in the depths of the forest of St. Germain. We
came upon it by chance and stopped at the gates, under the chestnut trees. To the right was an old well, to the left an iron gate—
open. We went in. The dull sound of footsteps on the moss-cov-
ered stones instantly filled me with emotion. At the first turning
I saw the semicircle formed by the great trees that surround the
château. By the outline of these masses against the sky I knew this
was the star I had been told about—a star of avenues, all leading
to this old hunting lodge of Louis XV.

Walking on, I stood before the curved façade with steps that
descended into a circular court. I saw the grace of the diminutive
paving stones, laid out in careful circles that extended as far as the
abandoned garden. This garden had retained its old design, made
by borders of box plants that enclosed the once-flowering beds,
now filled with a wild sea-green plant. In the heights of the forest
trees I heard the airy conversation of spring, and deeper in the
shadows shimmered the silver trunks of birch trees. The noble
semicircle that had so immediately moved me was composed of
chestnut trees. They had not yet put forth the thousands of white
bells that announce the arrival of summer, but their thick leaves
were massed on the boughs.

I stepped into the garden. The grass bore the imprint of a
horse's hooves, a child's ball lay under a bush, a handkerchief of
transparent mauve was caught on a bramble. The last light of the
sun was coming through the trees in pale slanting rays, a bird's
fragile call crystallized the silence, and everything gave off a per-
fume of antiquity. I felt that a future of enchanted moments was
waiting for me here in this hushed and fragrant forest.

The Château de la Muette, classed as an historic monument,
belonged to the Ministry of the Beaux Arts. No one had lived
in it for a long time. The Marquise de la Pompadour, one of its
ancient inhabitants, wrote to Voltaire: "The salons are splendid,
but the rest is nothing much." I admired indeed the three great

salons on the ground floor—the rotunda, lofty as the nave of a church, adorned with exquisite woodwork, its windows arched in that full curve that I love to the point of constructing it wherever I live; but "the rest" didn't disappoint me—on the contrary. I cannot live daily life with ease in great spaces, therefore the "nothing much" of la Pompadour had everything to charm me— low rooms, uneven ceilings, deep fireplaces, worn mirrors and closed alcoves that seemed made to hold dreams. The third floor, where it is said the Abbé Prévost wrote "Manon," pleased me still more—amusing mansard ceilings, walls formed by the exterior architecture and on the roof a wide terrace that advanced like a ship's prow over an ocean of trees. All the windows and doors, wide or narrow, disclosed sumptuous masses of forest.

The Muette was uninhabitable, therefore habitable for us. We rented it.

There was no gas, no electricity, no heating. An ancient stove refused to burn, a luxurious bathroom was without water.

The cracked faucets, the wall-paper peeling like eucalyptus trees, the holes in the roof showing the sky—all demanded enormous repairs. The Beaux Arts promised to undertake them. They deliberated the matter for two years.

Without waiting for repairs we moved in. We had the fundamentals—a well, candles and firewood. The doors and windows of the old château couldn't be tightly closed, so at night we felt unsafe, we needed a guardian.

On Christmas Eve, a night of snow and moonlight, a German police dog slipped into our kitchen. The color of over-done bread, and as ferocious as a wild beast, he had an incomprehensible charm. He understood that he must please us and he succeeded. I named him Thomas-the-Imposter.

Thomas had an exaggerated conception of his duty—in eighteen months he attempted to devour nine people. He retained from his former unknown life a hatred of man, a love of automobiles, a horror of cities and an adoration of women. Often he was only a dog, but at other times he disconcerted us with a certain expression, a human way of demanding attention and holding it. Then his bright nervous eyes became insistent and filled with melancholy. He begged for affection and clung to it with real distress.

The situation became acute. It was impossible to chain up such a creature and it was impossible to expose visitors to him any longer. I began to search for a comfortable home for my dear friend, what he needed was a widow with a large walled-in property. After weeks of vain inquiries, Thomas's death became imperative. A few hours before the time set for execution a premonition made me return to the veterinarian. There I found a woman who was demanding for that very night a watchdog that had bitten at least several people. Her husband had just died and she herself was dying of fright in her château—a property comprising four acres surrounded by walls. Evidently Thomas had been born under a lucky star . . .

The nights in the forest of the Muette were of a complex magnificence. We could not resist exploring their secret shadows—we needed to share the solitude of the earth, listen to the breathing of the sleeping trees, distinguish little by little the furtive forms of rabbits or squirrels, terrified at our approach. Nights of fog were still more secret. The shrouded forest was visible only where an impetuous branch had torn aside the mist. Its smell stung our throats, its vapors drenched our hair, we brought it home clinging to our clothes. On such nights the forest held a treachery that made one think of the sea.

Sometimes, protected by the shadows, deer came out to play around the villa. We heard their trotting steps approach, breaking the little branches in their path. The youngest hind came bounding, as if late for a rendezvous. On moonlight nights they played and danced, animating this abandoned place with scenes of grace; then all at once they were seized with panic and took flight, darting away together. The shadows absorbed them, nothing remained but the moon and its serenity.

We would then go indoors, guided by a lamp in a window. We crossed the rotunda where my big crystal ball monopolized the light. It has been with me always and has defied the destiny of fragile things. Shining and flawless, I see it in my memory as it reflected each year the multicolored light of a Christmas tree.

Dreams and their Language

It was at the Muette and the lighthouse that I wrote "Souvenirs." (Volume I: My Life with Maeterlinck*)

During the years since my return from America, I had felt like an automobile with its motor racing at a hundred miles an hour in a closed garage. I began slowly to realize that I was not yet in a proper state to begin a new life. I was running away from something, I was still fleeing from a suffering which I couldn't cure because I didn't yet understand it. One day a friend said to me, "You'll never recover your equilibrium until you've ruthlessly analyzed your past, and the best way to do that is to write about it." I agreed, but I knew that it would be profoundly painful and I waited five years before beginning my book. How could I have written it sooner? For years I had felt that I was dragging after me a corpse larger than myself—the corpse of my dead life, a life I had given away and that had returned to me after twenty years. How long and difficult they were, those after-years in which I had to create a perspective in the center of an endless tragedy—a tragedy of astonishment. Oh, to live on was simple—implacable Nature takes care of that. But to live a new life was not simple. As in a film one has seen many times, I saw myself making the same mistakes, adopting the same "ideals," beginning the same

---

* This book bore no relation to the memoirs that had appeared in the *Sunday American*, and the Dodd Mead edition was never published.

cycles. Every day I forced myself to revise and discard. Suspended between my dead past and my unconceived future, I fell between the two. I knew the special agony of a being lost in time
who could no longer accept herself. It was then that I went to
America, where I began to speak, to think, in two mingled lan-
guages. Emerging from my native speech, I moved in a new space.
I breathed again.

It was now ten years since my separation from Maeterlinck.
I have a slow-motion heart, I do not know what it is to forget,
nor do I believe it possible. The four-footed animal doesn't forget, nor does the human animal; only the latter doesn't like to
admit it. Some people wish to bury the past, but it haunts them;
some vilify it; some ridicule it. Some people drag their pasts behind them without knowing it; others nourish the disarray of
their sorrow and cling to it because they have natures that have
stopped like clocks—they are the false inconsolables, greatly admired by the world. None of this is real. In every case the ability
to forget seems to me an invention.

I finished "Souvenirs" in Paris, in 1932, and it was published by
Bernard Grasset. Unfortunately Grasset chose to launch it with
an introduction by himself into which he inserted the idea that
the book was a revindication on my part. "Revindication" is one
of those words to which calumny rushes and clings. This deform-
ing preface, concealed from me until the day of publication, was
also built on the idea that the love story revealed in "Souvenirs"
was not a great love but merely a literary love.

A literary love? Mon Dieu, if I had really been able to bridge
the hiatus that exists between life and poetry, to love as in a poem,
without allowing the corrosion of life to tarnish the conception
of the poet . . . this is indeed what I had wanted, what I had tried
to do.

Each life begins with the same choice before it—to follow one's parents or one's dreams. Like all artists, I was born closer to my dreams than to the world. The destiny of dreams includes every catastrophe. But the world does not tell us what we will gain by dreaming, it doesn't know. That remains our sumptuous secret—a secret that depends on the stakes for which we play and the totality of the risks we take.

In spite of the vagueness of dreams and the grace which they bestow, I had needed to give a certain form to my secret life. I loved it too much to limit it to my personality and its turmoils; I tried to construct it, chisel it like an object, to conform to my idea. Formed by dreams and their language, the artist creates in the material world the super-normal life which is his oxygen. He does not live by illusion or delusion, as is believed, but by the affirmations of the sun within him.

All poets have expressed their love. Veiled or not, it is visible. One may dislike the manner or form of its revealment, but who would dare to disfigure its emotion even if it seemed impossible or absurd? Even at the infamous trial of Wilde, when the stolid British Jury was judging "the love which dares not speak its name," they dared not say, "the love which did not exist."

It was this criterion that defined the exact nature of the shock I received on reading Grasset's preface. It was the curious case of a publisher interpreting an author according to his own private psychology. The act, though not serious in itself, hurt me severely. I knew that a sacrilege had been committed. I forced myself to reread Grasset's words. I read them with the tips of my eyes, and my revolt rose to a point that made my life tremble. Why should I suffer so because a Grasset had misinterpreted me? Was it my vanity that was wounded? No, my vanity is greater than that.

But the fact that my life's story should be associated with the vulgarity of soul that emanated from Grasset's pages embarrassed me to the point of repugnance. To stop the sale of the book I consulted Moro-Giafferi, the celebrated lawyer. To my stupefaction he tried to convince me that I was wrong. "But you haven't read the book," I said, "I have no bitterness; it's idiotic." His taut face crinkled into a cabbage, he held out the palms of his hands; his long practice of manipulating in the void helped him to find arguments for Grasset's defense. I listened to his voice, an instrument on which he played like a virtuoso; I watched his mouth with its Louis XVI curves, and I understood that he could scarcely see me through the fog of his own importance. Of course he and Grasset were of the same opinion—for them there could be no love where there was neither possessiveness nor scenes of jealousy. With this bourgeois preface they could raise their arms high like comrades, they could "come down to earth," "be themselves" again, resume the familiar sniffings of a dog-to-dog humanity.

In any case my position was hopeless as I had not stipulated, in writing, that the preface should be submitted to me before publication. I decided that I would trust my book to the understanding of the public, knowing that human instinct always understands three elementals that have an unchanging greatness—life, love, death. So I accepted the publication and wrote in all the copies sent to the press: "Please judge this book on what it contains, not on the preface."

I learned later that the copies thus signed had been destroyed on Grasset's order.

Four Days of Snow

It was arranged that I should drive to Paris every day, to Grasset's offices in the rue des St. Pères, to sign all press copies, since I had accepted the situation, there was nothing to do but follow its mechanism.

The first morning as I left the Muette it was snowing. The forest was a scene of marble and the trees of the bridle paths formed solid porticos against the sky. The car advanced over a crust of ice that crackled like mica. For once the forest and the snow were only an empty landscape to me—the partitions of my being were emptied of everything but sound, like the feeling that comes after a fall.

Once again, in a time of sorrow, the pale snow was falling and I remembered another day of snow . . . in a Paris street four years ago. I was stepping from a taxi to the curb when there passed, close to me, almost touching my cape, a person I had not seen for the centuries that follow a final separation. Standing motionless, without breathing, I felt all my blood flowing away at my feet. Maeterlinck stopped farther on before the window of a bookshop. I overtook him. Against the dark bindings of the books the glass reflected his face, I saw him as in still water. I wanted to say, "How are you?"—meaning for him to hear, "What has become of your life, the life one does not see?" But we stood side by side in silence—he not seeing, I seeing too much; seeing so well that I let him go his way, fearing he might reply, "Very well, and you?"

As I entered the Grasset offices, columns of packages of "Souvenirs" greeted me. On a table beside them were stacked the wrappers in which each book was to be enclosed: "A woman gave her life and began to regret it."

Snow was falling in the narrow court, in front of the glass enclosed office where I sat writing my dedications. Several authors passed by and came in to offer their condolences for the catastrophe of the preface. "But you are wrong to suffer about it," Jacques Chardonne said. "It doesn't matter at all. At first I was opposed to the idea of your book, but the moment I began to read it I loved it." Grasset stood in the corridor, a dead cigarette extending beyond his profile. He is supposed to have an intimidating back; it is merely a back full of assurance, like that of a sergeant snapping out commands. Finally he came in to say, "Listen, Georgette Leblanc, I didn't think you would be so angry. You certainly haven't waited all your life to be tricked by me. You must be used to it by now."

People can be divided into those who trick and those who are tricked. To trick eats up all one's time, and besides one must keep one's eyes eternally fixed on the ground, like a chicken. I could have protected myself against Grasset's trickery by carrying my vanity before me as a shield, like the people who cry, "You can do these things to other people but you can't do them to me!" Such people are respected, like the walls on which it is forbidden to paste advertisements. But I too have a protection—it is my lightning rod destiny. Those who sympathize with my misadventures would be consoled if they realized that the lightning rod, not myself, receives the full shock of my life's disasters.

Two years had scarcely passed when we had to give up the Muette. As soon as the first repairs were finished the rent was raised. Moreover, the Beaux Arts planned to arrange the château for the Council President's weekends, thus making it and its haunting charm an accessory of the Republic.

A year ago, in the late autumn, I returned to the Muette one day. A whirl of dead leaves welcomed me. I saw again the young wisteria, but the sound of bees no longer came from its clusters. Farther along, on the north wall, I could almost see the invisible flowers which, in summer, color the old stones as they did in the cloister I loved. As I stood on the perron the memory of an evening's party came back to me: darkness had taken possession of skies and forms; on a table pink roses lay in a bowl; candle flames, blown by a breeze, formed chains of wax tears that clung to the candelabra, diffusing an odor of tapers and oblivion.

For the last time I looked down the long avenue of chestnut trees towering above me like high walls of gold. From time to time a golden leaf floated down in a slow spiral, returning gently to the earth.

CHAPTER SIX
LETTERS TO A YOUNG STUDENT

THE years passed quickly... In 1935 circumstances permitted me to see Gurdjieff constantly, often daily.

As time went on, the material of my former life had begun to recede. It was my first life, the life none of us knows how to live except in disorder and bewilderment. I was now ready to give all my energy to those conditions which Gurdjieff had named as the terms of development. It was not easy. I felt like a bird tapping to get out of its shell. What lay beyond, for me, would be as different as the world outside the shell would be for the bird.

I was slowly changing, and sometimes I was afraid of no longer recognizing myself, between the non-existent image which had been my companion and this new image that I barely saw, a fog was rising. In it both images were obliterated and I pursued them blindly, afraid of finding neither.

Often I wanted to escape, to turn away from this super-science which demanded too much of me. Yet escape seemed criminal, as well as impossible. A truth once perceived, even for a second, is never lost; it comes to light again in spite of everything. And if one wants to live this truth, one realizes that one has been promised to it, that all the events of a lifetime have been converging toward it.

1936 arrived... The writing of "Souvenirs" and the continuous effort demanded in working with Gurdjieff had helped me to emerge from my tragedy of astonishment.

To clarify myself further, I tried again to write. I wanted my new book to be a simplification of life and its motivations, not a literary book made with words considered appropriate to such material. After months of effort, of daily rejection of phrases that recurred in a sickening pattern of literature, I stopped. To cure this sickness I began to write a series of letters to a young friend who had always enjoyed asking me questions on those subjects I most liked to talk about.

Writing

I shall try to talk to you in letters as I do when I am with you. When I talk with you I am aided by your attention—you know how to listen. Though it is always easy for me to talk, a terrible anguish seizes me when I try to write—at least to write for the public. How can I destroy this anguish? I want to write as I write letters, as I talk with one person, not with people. Writing to a friend is a liberation for me, I see the "chose de vie" coming to life on paper. It is this "thing of life" that I desire above and beyond everything. It is the blood of words. To transfuse it onto paper is the most difficult problem of my present life, even more difficult than living without anything to live on.

I must try to express myself once and for all as if, should I fail, the penalty would be electrocution. I must at last express myself without using a single inflated word. Ah! Those words inflated like balloons, they are at the root of my suffering. I have come to realize their emptiness and that is the reason I have fallen into this strangling, speechless state. To have become mute, I, who breathe only through exultation! That is why this morning I threw myself upon this sheet of paper, to talk to you, I will not leave this letter until I have said all I must say.

Always, from all the people who have lived close to me, I have heard the same plea: "Write as you talk." What prevents me from doing it? The effort I am now making is so torturing to me that my heart pounds, my throat is closed, my hands burn like white coals. Why, why all this? Because the moment to finish this book has come, because I must give out the too-much that is in me—that too-much which I used to send out over the footlights. But now I must give more than in any theatre, because there is at stake my soul itself, made of all I have lived, felt, understood, loved and hated. All this is fermenting in my mind, you see, and I can no longer endure it.

Most writers have one personality on paper and another in life. I discovered this when I was very young. Later, when I began to labor over the craft of writing, Maeterlinck told me that I would never develop a technique unless I gave up my insistence on being real, exactly myself. "You must create a double for yourself, it is more urgent than a style. You are as serious as a donkey, and you have the obsession of authenticity. Make your 'double' carefree and superficial, then he will help you." He called words the "cement." "One small idea should suffice for an article," he used to say; "on this idea you construct hypotheses and cement them with words to infinity. That is the way to work." I didn't try. To me an article should be like a foot-bridge—a solid plank for each step. I preferred to follow the advice of Anatole France: "Live, love as much as possible, then you will write." "But it may be too late," I said. "There is plenty of time to bore oneself," he said, his black silk cap quivering on his skull. Madame de Caillavet came in—she had heard the last words. Her eye, that of a hen of the grand siècle, flayed the pitiful Anatole who quickly ran down like a top. "Don't listen to him, he's only a lazybones," she said, dropping her words as if they were red-hot. Then she left the room, delighted to have spoiled Anatole's pleasure. He murmured, embarrassed, "She's right, without her I wouldn't work at all."

Writers of novels disguise their true selves, yet it is easy to recognize them under their make-up. But the minds of essayists, moralists and philosophers, when they write, seem to look through a pane of colored glass which fades when their work is done. In my youth the letters of Flaubert meant more to me than his books. I was advised to read the letters of Madame de Sévigné and I detested them. Later on I could analyze the process of this fabricated naturalness. It is simian—or would be if a monkey could write with talent in imitation of man and the nature of man. The letters of Madame de Sévigné are but an excuse to play

to the gallery—pirouettes, ronds de jambes, garlands of the epoch, verve, sparkle, cleverness. That is why they could not satisfy
me. Always, in all things and at all ages, I have been impressed
only by life—simple and all-powerful life.

In 1908 Colette wrote to me, apropos my first book, *The Choice
of life:* "But I won't dare talk with you anymore. You say, 'We lose
nothing when a desolating truth takes the place of a beautiful illusion.' Will I ever be able to think so nobly? No, I even believe
I would be sad. You must forgive me but I lack, among so many
other things, the 'need for knowledge.' To be half ignorant, to
fear, to disdain, to desire passionately (but without perseverance),
to detest and to curse (to the point of blows)—this is the fate to
which I must be left. I have been astonished—forgive me, yes,
astonished—by the inexhaustible force one feels in you. I wish
you were queen of something or somewhere—people would be
astounded."

As for Colette's writing, the technical schooling that Willy
imposed on her was simple and objective, with vacuous meta-
phors forbidden. Also, Colette is essentially a conformist. When
she is not writing divinely about nature and animals, her pattern
holds her close to social life, the life that is lived by everyone. It
is here that her great talent lies, in a world that bores me but to
which she gives of her energy as in a blood transfusion. Her char-
acters are more alive in her pages than in life, where they think of
nothing but their own petty affairs.

Colette is not separated from her talent. That is her force, and
it is characteristic of the greatest women writers. My sole ambition is to identify myself as closely as possible with my material.
Am I doing it in this letter? I don't know. I have left off and taken
it up again twice, without rereading. I suppose there is wastage in
it, as in talk, but does it matter? I want to look further than that.

I want to write as I see, as I speak. I see before I think. It is this
function that suggests poems to me. When I draw, the first line
expresses the salient characteristic—a living person is there on

the paper. The line shows the person as a word should represent a thought—no artificial form encloses the idea, only the one created by the material itself, its size and its structure.

Mon Dieu! If I should count the hours, the days, the years, I have spent sitting before a blank page of paper, they would add up to a lifetime. It is like having lived in a glass bowl, revolving, without being able to break through the crystal globe. Even when I ceased my whirling struggles I remained a prisoner of them. Don't think I am exaggerating. My efforts to write were in proportion to my need; without that need to express myself I would long ago have given up the struggle. I have trunks of manuscripts and have published only five books. You may wonder how I was able to finish "Souvenirs." The answer is simple—I had signed a contract, agreed to a publication date. All that is worth anything in the book welled up in me at rare moments, due no doubt to some unconscious pressure of nature; the rest was achieved with difficulty, slowly, as if it were being torn from me. Either I advanced or I was blocked. When I advanced the writing was immediate, content and form were one, there was nothing that I could arrange afterward. When I was blocked, it was the terrifying glass bowl again, and the frantic whirling.

Am I suddenly liberated, or shall I discover in these pages the restriction I hate and that I never feel when a poem comes to me, forms in me, and goes out from me quite simply? A poem, to me, is a sorrow that rises and descends. It depends on a vision, in which I see the sorrow like a picture drawn by my nerves. Why not write prose with the same simplicity? I do not know.

Margaret often says, "Write what you have just said to me, it is full of personal information."

Since my nature has not diminished, since time has slowed down nothing in me, I should, I must, be able to express myself as I wish. I must find a way to write simply and easily about the subject matter which passionately interests me—personal information.

Singing

Today I should like to talk about the mysterious substance that is called Art.

You tell me that Madame B., the singer, is an artist. I am shocked, as I used to be before I knew why I suffered when listening to good singers who lacked all sense of art. To be a good singer or a good musician is not necessarily a more subtle matter than to be a good cook.

You add that Madame B. lives like an artist. But appearances have nothing to do with it; and what does that mean—to "live like an artist"? Think of Mallarmé—outwardly a man like any other, a modest professor of English whom no one would have noticed in a crowd. But the hours I spent with him, in the little room where he worked, are unique in my memory. Seated at a fragile writing-table, a scotch shawl over his shoulders, he explained to me his theory of the written language. I only half understood; at twenty it was difficult and I was too dazzled by his mind. But I was conscious of being in the presence of one of the rarest artists who ever lived.

I know nothing of the life of Madame B. and have no desire to know more. It is enough to hear her sing the first measures of a song to know that she will go as on wheels to the end and that nothing will "arrive." You understand me? With the born artist something always arrives. A world of new emotion knocks you breathless and leaves you unconscious of everything except it.

When I was twelve, in Rouen, I had a little pianist friend, slightly younger than I, who was a "prodigy," she played the most complicated Beethoven sonatas, and all Chopin without blinking. Her dimpled hands had to cheat in order to hurdle the arpeggios. Small and round, she was hoisted on to a pile of piano scores and immediately began to play, her fingers scratching the keys in a frenzy. Crouched over the keyboard of an immense concert piano, curved far forward and dressed in pink silk, she made me think of a shrimp. All her family, clothed in black, sat very straight on the Louis Philippe chairs that were grouped around the Pleyel. The "connoisseurs" in the audience exchanged glances when the child's virtuosity carried her over perilous passages. These people were what are called good people; they helped the poor and praised themselves for their charitable deeds. I found them hard and redoubtable, like all the people in the city of my birth.

Nelly-Rose and I were the little phenomena of Rouen. Our parents even wanted us to give a public concert—"At that age an exhibition carries no consequences." Unfortunately I showed no enthusiasm. They could not see why and were annoyed with me.

I waited my turn to sing, my anguish increasing as I listened to Nelly-Rose's playing. These moments for me were filled with a painful mystery. Suddenly she stopped. The parents applauded, then turned their eyes on me. I placed my music in front of Nelly-Rose and at once her fingers went to work. This haste upset me, I wanted her to look at me and wait. To my plea she always replied, "Mamma says that looks affected," and played even faster. Our first song was Mozart's "Mon Coeur Soupire," which I adored. I slipped into the delicate melody as if it were a crystal sphere, and here was the piano smashing everything. I tried to continue, I controlled my tears. My despair increased until the moment when the grandmother—it was always she who spoke first because she had sung in her youth—rose and declared in a crisp voice, "My children, it is not good. You must practice, we will leave you."

I knew that no amount of practicing would be of any use. Immediately Nelly-Rose began to justify herself—"But I played what was written." She repeated the first measures, but never as I wanted; and what I wanted I could not express. I stopped singing. Nelly-Rose became exasperated. "I who play the most difficult pieces! You don't know what you want, it's your fault, always your fault!" She ran away in one direction, I in the other. I hid in the somber park, so thick with trees that spring could never penetrate it. The young green leaves looked grey, all the paths descended to the Seine and there was a very old smell of mold and water. I had the double sorrow of not knowing exactly what my sorrow was. I wanted to find the necessary words to explain this "other thing" that for me was everything, but I could find no words. I felt that I was alone in the world. I wept.

For months I suffered from this mystery. One day Nelly-Rose's father told mine that his family found me too artiste and would not allow her to see me anymore. I was stricken. My first feeling of tenderness had been for her, my grief demanded a farewell. Nelly-Rose knew my despair. I sent word to her that I would pass two or three times each day before her window, that she should lift the curtain if she was a little sad.

But the curtain never moved. Thus I understood that she was not like me, and that we could not understand each other in life any more than in music.

The great difference between the mechanism of art and art itself was soon to be revealed to me. It was Isabel, my second friend, who with her sumptuous nature brought me the living revelation of "the artist"—the revelation for which I had been waiting.

She was a little girl "Rimbaud" who died in her youth, killed by the excess that was in her. Dazzled by her own knowledge and knowing nothing that can be taught, she arrived on earth with an innocence which her later anger and disdain intensified. Born an artist, with extraordinary and multiple gifts, she lived without expressing them, seeming to understand that her time would be too brief. She was a true phenomenon who shunned the role of phenomenon.

She could be seen on her balcony, in her garden, as tragically idle as a prisoner. In the street she seemed not to walk but rather to bound into the wind like an archangel, hair streaming, hands empty. She was the evocation of an element, an unleashed spirit, yet she was a frail child who was soon to die.

I had not imagined that one could distinguish so clearly the brief passage of a spirit among humans. Her world was not here. She came only to leave again, like a traveller who has arrived in the wrong country. She was born divinely lost and with a heart suffocated by love. She gave me that magnificent heart and disappeared. All my life I was to feel upon me the guardian light of this prodigious child.

The establishment of Klein, the well-known music publisher of Rouen, was in the rue Gantré, one of the oldest and darkest streets of the town. The walls were discolored and the pavement muddy, as if it were always raining there. This street was only a short distance from the Solferino Gardens where my governess took me every day to play with a swarm of adolescents of my own age who raced about noisily, raising clouds of dust. I was fifteen and it was April. Gardeners were setting out tulips, new leaves smelled like flowers, the trees were filled with birds and covered with sunlight. But I ran away, leaving the light of the garden for the darkness of the rue Gantré. Here I entered an old shop. Its broken bell tinkled a single note, there was a smell of dust and shadow, and the two old clerks sitting by the door did not lift their faces from their ledgers. I went directly to the rear of the shop and into a little green velvet salon where my old friend, the père Klein, had his office.

He looked like Verlaine except for a covering of thick white hair. His little eyes were buried in a nest of wrinkles and he wore a quilted jacket and large felt slippers. He had surrounded himself with portraits of contemporary celebrities—photographs signed with flourishes and explosive dedications, for his music shop was the meeting place of the artists of all countries. He himself was an artist and gave me lessons on the organ, having conquered my father's opposition by talking of mystical vibrations which would develop my religious feelings. All the hours I could steal from the

Solferino Gardens I spent in the good père Klein's shop. How he laughed, seeing me arrive breathless, radiant, clutching my music to my heart. I went up the great staircase leading to the music room, which smelled of furniture polish, and passed between two hedges of glistening pianos that led to the concert hall. There I jumped upon the stage and accompanied myself for hours, in a frenzy at hearing my voice ring out in its full strength.

One day—it was the thirteenth of April—Klein announced that he had a surprise for me. He led me upstairs and told me to sing and keep on singing, even if someone should come into the room. Before long a man appeared in the doorway. He was rather small, with a grey moustache, a soft hat set on the back of his head and a travelling coat thrown over his shoulders. He was clapping his hands and I recognized him from my postcard collection of musicians—it was Massenet! Père Klein stood beaming behind him. Massenet immediately sat down at the piano and began playing "Manon." I sang "N'est-ce ma main?"... and it was as if I were outside myself, as if I were singing in a dream. Massenet gave me the cues as we sang together. At the end he rushed into the arms of the père Klein shouting, "It is Vaillant-Couturier I find again! The same passion, the same diction!" And the père Klein exulted, "I told you so! I knew! I knew!" Massenet began another scene and I sang again—I knew all the roles of the opera. I sang as if I had come alive for the first time. Massenet kept repeating, "Why do I find in this child all the passion of Vaillant-Couturier?" I said, "Why do you find that strange? I suppose that when she was fifteen Mme. Vaillant-Couturier already had what she had later." "Ah!" Massenet cried, embracing père Klein again. She has a brain too, cette petite!"

Hours passed, the windows turned deep blue and the light of a street lamp entered the room. I had a moment of panic, for I had to be at home before my father arrived. We found my coat and hat and I ran down the stairs. Massenet called after me, "A demain! Tomorrow we will continue. You are a great artist!"

I ran through the streets, intoxicated and delirious, my knees trembling. The guardian of the Solferino gate was ringing the evening bell for closing time. I found my governess who was flirting in the *kiosque des plaisirs* and we ran home together, five minutes later I was dining opposite my father. Under the light of the hanging-lamp I lowered my eyes, half dead, strangled with happiness.

My life had begun. Massenet had given me the certainty of possessing a treasure which would last as long as my life itself.

Accompanying

Years afterward I remember Massenet telling me, "In Paris you will find many pianists to accompany you as I do." He was mistaken. I found stupid "followers" who called themselves "supple," or impetuous martinets who called themselves "leaders." I met hundreds of Nelly-Roses, but in a whole lifetime only six or seven artist-musicians who possessed the inexplicable science of accompaniment. One must be more than a musician, more than a virtuoso, whether an accompanist considers himself a follower or a leader, no communication is possible if he lacks the very essence of life—electricity. Massenet's personal electricity was overwhelming. It constituted both his charm and the great youthfulness which outrode his age for long years.

To be an accompanist like Massenet, it is not enough to have long experience or even the most perfect talent. One must be in electrical correspondence with the singer and control or submit to the slightest change in the ebb and flow of the two interacting currents. I do not imagine that Massenet—in life as at the piano—met many currents that remained hostile to his. But he was an extremely modest man. When I cried, entranced, "Oh, maître, your accompaniment is unique, unique!" he replied gently, "My child, it is you and I together—I do not accompany everyone in the same way."

Walter Straram, another musician-accompanist I found later, played in frescoes. With him, Debussy's "Le Balcon" and "La Mort des Amants" unfurled in enormous waves. Straram conceived and played on the grand scale. One saw as much as one heard, even details took on horizons. This man looked like a gruesome marionette, a burned man; he seemed to crackle in flames. His refusal to compromise was royal. If he heard people exchanging ideas which did not please him, he cut them with his wit as a diamond cuts glass. A certain twist of his mouth revealed his contempt for the whole earth. One day I said to him, "Scorn people, yes, but things . . ." He closed his teeth, "People! That is not enough friend, not enough. Things—they are already half people."

I knew him when he was poor and obscure, known only to a few musicians who believed in him. We left together for Boston—he wanted to go, and I wanted only him for accompanist, when I returned to Europe he stayed on in America. Ten years later I found him again in Paris, known everywhere and living luxuriously. I went to two of the concerts he conducted in the Salle Gaveau. They were academic—and I had expected him to be a clairvoyant on the platform. Later I met him in a salon and found no resemblance to the man who, ten years before, was often called mad. We saw each other several times but always in "society," which deforms everything that has a real existence. That certain twist of the mouth was still there, but his magnificent intransigence was frozen.

André Caplet, another great musician, was also a great accompanist. When he touched the piano there was magic around him. People had always described him as the ugliest man in the world and when I met him for the first time I was amazed that a man could have features without line or color and still be so charming. It is said that to be sympathetic is the secret of charm. That is not true; one can be sympathetic without being hypnotic. It is the presence of charm that produces magic. André Caplet's playing was permeated with his surprising charm. He played as the cat walks, with a padded technique, the musical design very precise and indicated through detail. Debussy always said, "Caplet, he *is* my music."

Octave Maus accompanied beautifully in spite of his perfect musicianship. You are shocked by that "in spite of"? I have no respect for musicianship for its own sake—it can be bought, while art is always given. But Octave Maus was not limited by his knowledge, because he was a master-colorist. He played as Van Gogh painted. His active eyes saved him from a virtuosity which might have outshone the color at the tips of his fingers.

I really remember only those people who have touched me either emotionally or aesthetically. When they have done both, as Charles Bordes did, the images that remain in my memory are like bright paintings.

How I loved Bordes! He was a god at the piano—a god with unknotted cravat, shiny coat and a useless arm, for he was paralyzed on the right side.

I can still see him the first time he came up the lane of yellow roses leading to our villa in Grasse, falling from one leg to the other, his left hand waving to me as if we already knew each other. No two temperaments could have been more alike than ours— I knew it as soon as he sat at the piano, accomplishing marvels with his one hand. He had come to coach me in the opera "Castor and Pollux," which we were to produce ourselves in Montpellier. I can still feel the enthusiasm as we filled with an identical rhythm the silent spaces that Rameau's music allowed us. There were no dead silences in our conception, any more than in the composer's. Bordes would say, "You are right, there is no explanation for these things nor any school for teaching the essential. Either you live Rameau or you do not." We believed that there were no *laws* for the classical, but a single law which is rectitude ... the arrangement of Greek columns in the sky of Athens, all life contained in a frame of perfection.

Bordes was always in a state of exaltation which made this half a man more complete than others; but he always looked as if he were in mourning—head shaved and covered with a black shadow, magnificent black eyes, a suit of black cloth and a narrow black tie. How clearly I remember him at the concert of his songs we gave together in Montpellier, as he limped across the stage, his shyness vanquished by love of music. The first time he accompanied me in his "Gigue," the Verlaine poem he had set to music, tears rolled down his cheeks. "I thought I would die," he wept, "without ever hearing my 'Gigue' as I hear it inside myself."

Reynaldo Hahn captivates his audience as soon as he sits down at the piano. His accompaniment is an atmosphere, an envelopment. And it is not only his charm that operates, it is also his musical science which he never displays. He wraps his power in nonchalance, and he can sing like a nightingale while smoking cigarettes.

Once when he was accompanying me in public I leaned toward him before beginning his "Infidélité" and said, "I usually make some changes in this song, but tonight ..." He stopped me. "It will be very amusing on the contrary. Let us see." Not many composers have so little amour propre.

I have often wondered whether the exasperations of daily life ever shattered Reynaldo's perfect self-control. I don't believe so. One day I watched him in a struggle with an orchestra from which he could extract nothing. Returning to the wings, he mopped his forehead with a calm hand and smiled. But his eyes were darker in his pale face and when he said in a quiet voice, "I shall be obliged to change the program," I was interested to see that nothing betrayed the exasperation he was feeling.

Paul Dukas, whose energy at the piano was of the highest voltage, was concentrated and in focus. Nothing in him overflowed, nothing reached out, even his features were withdrawn. But it is the mystery of rare people that what they conceal, rather than what they show, reveals them. I must have annoyed him sometimes with my enthusiasm, yet our accord was basically perfect. I remember a certain pause I asked him for, in the "Ariane" music, which would give me time to clarify the enigmatic character of Ariane for the public. At first he was puzzled—the precision of his writing left nothing to chance; but when I explained my reasons he accepted them, surprised not to have thought of them himself.

Once I asked him what enjoyment he found in certain sonatas which to me are like congealed life. He answered, "One is interested in following the construction, in hearing the same theme turned and twisted in a dozen ways."

"But what is the interest of that?" I asked. "If an artist turned his model in every direction I would see it lengthwise, sidewise, head down, feet in air, and so? . . . I don't call that creation. Such variations only make me feel that I am listening to a gossip of vibrations."

Teaching

I love to teach singing—you have the impression of creating even the pupil himself. Singing is the expression of a nature; it contains the soul, its quality, its audible unfolding. This is why singing is intolerable unless there is "someone" within the singer. More often than not there is no one; sometimes there is someone who is inhibited or imprisoned. In such a case the task goes beyond teaching and becomes creation. The teaching of singing is in reality a school of "being." But the element of divinity in the human voice is seldom the preoccupation of singing teachers. Many beautiful voices are ruined after a few years of use. Born in space and made for it, they are slowly suffocated by a life lived for material things alone. Knowing this, one understands why certain voices remain young in a body that grows old. Voices that are destroyed by time are "matter." The ones that are spirit remain as long as life itself.

Singing for singing's sake has never stirred me. It is the person I look for behind the voice that preoccupies me. A voice in a concert hall, a bell in the sky are beautiful, but that is not what I mean. Nor do I mean the miracle of vocalizations in a throat—I prefer the nightingale. And yet if he were isolated from his season, his trees and moons, his first flutings in cold twilights, I think I would no longer love him.

What moves me is not singing, but music; not the instrument but the art. Ah, the rapture of what I have known as art! From the day when I first thought of my voice as a medium for this rapture, my life turned and followed after it. In America, when I had nothing to live on, it fed my life and its own.

Drawing

My eyes forget nothing that they have loved. They are museums. I visit them when I am tired or ill and they are a guarantee of felicity. Because of them I have never been bored by waiting for a person or a train—I can always go wherever I like without moving. I do not have to read magazines at the dentist's, for my museum is with me—more crowded each minute. I see a smile, the nape of a neck, a glance, a walk, and I see hands—hands full of fear, hands that are modest, hands that destroy.

In my museum I love to visit an animal gallery which honors it. A certain little cat is there. She has nothing of what is called remarkable. Dressed in a little grey and white suit, trimmed in black, her appearance is unassuming. She does not attract attention in the street, but she fills our rooms with charm. We never tire of her attraction or her eyes, which are sad at this moment because she has just come to know love, when she is at peace they are yellow or green. Now they have a troubled concentration and a too-beautiful distress. Questions without answers.

My eyes love to look. People who please me have only to sit down before me in silence—just to look at them overcomes me with delight. Conversely, it is natural that my eyes should suffer. They would like to discover in faces a little modesty, a little restraint, or at least an uneasiness. Why are so many people pleased with their defects? Why do they not try to correct them, or at least keep them in the background?

When I was a child my parents forced me to go out on Saturdays in curlpapers so that on Sunday I would have two frizzy rolls on either side of my head. For my birthday present I chose an umbrella with an enormous ugly handle. I held it in front of me on Saturdays and it was a shield—people looked at the ugliness of the umbrella and didn't see mine.

My eyes anger me by seeing everything, and I should like to stop them up like ears. It is difficult to prevent them from recording every detail without discrimination. Therefore when I draw I see my model better if he is not present. The perfect conditions for me to make a good caricature are to be alone, to be tired, to feel like laughing and to draw in a dim light. If the pencil needs sharpening, then everything is favorable and I put on paper a portrait so amazingly lifelike that I am the first to be struck by it. Whatever it is—caricature, sketch or portrait—I cannot say that I think, plan or imagine. I only see. But I see with all my strength.

I can draw any face except a beloved face. There, something restrains me. I think the obstacle is in my brain, for the act seems a little sacrilegious to me. What I love cannot be put on paper, nor can my reason for loving. I cannot create with a line what is to me a world.

Acting

What, exactly, is acting? To enter into a state of excitement, to release all one's nature, to let oneself go.

All my life, whenever I have walked on to a stage, I have thought, "What happiness, I am going to let myself go." I have never seen an engine letting off steam without thinking, "That is just what I do in the theatre—I make it loud or soft and that's all there is to it," for this reason I have been happier acting than singing.

To me schools of acting, rules of acting, all methods of teaching acting, are unimportant.

Art is a state. As the state of grace makes saints, so the state of art makes the artist—a soil which produces what other soils will never produce. The act of art is only a consequence—an infinite consequence if its source is authentic, nothing if it comes only from a profession or ambition.

I used to believe that drama was the greatest of the arts. It seemed to contain all the others—prose, poetry, painting, sculpture. I think now that the art of the actor is the most inferior, the vainest and most obvious form of exhibitionism. And it is because the springs of this passion have always been in my cells that I am able to examine them, it is the violence of this appetite that pulls an actor from his bed in spite of suffering. Physically I have very little endurance, yet I have endured any torture on the stage. The worst toothache has been abolished by the anesthesia of the footlights. Once I sang a whole act of an opera with a tack in my foot. The tack went in deeper with each step but I never dreamed of limping. The intolerable pain was tolerable until the moment when I fainted in the wings. This was not courage or willpower—

it would have been an act of courage to leave the stage and have the curtain lowered.

If the actor when acting is like a drunkard when intoxicated, how does he regulate his frenzy? His automatism does this for him. We are perpetually automatic in our lives, and naturally no less so in the theatre. An actress like Duse understood this and told me that she came on the stage only at the last rehearsal in order not to lose her spontaneity. She knew the force of automatism and so feared its dangers that she constructed her roles entirely in her bed, thus saving her strength and keeping her impressions and reflexes intact.

The sincerity of the actor is a subject of eternal discussion. Since sincerity can only be relative, why talk of it at all? Talma, in order to arrive on the stage in a state of fury, would first throw himself upon anyone who happened to be standing in the wings. He raged, roared and reddened, then ran on stage like a madman. The public exulted in such a perfect, such an authentic sincerity.

This copy of emotion which I find repellent, is the exact type of sincerity possible to the theatre. It is this false sincerity that Stanislavski cultivated in his Moscow Art Theatre. He would ask an actor to come on the stage under the shock of some terrible news and to translate this state into any words at all, simply to make the springs of his emotion function. The actor had to do this over and over, arrive at the paroxysm of his emotion without thinking of his words. Stanislavski made a human being a dynamo charged and obedient to the slightest command. At that time I admired this method of work. I see today that it represents precisely the harm done to the actor by his profession. He emerges psychically attacked, his sympathetic nervous system exhausted. The actor is always unbalanced in life, crippled from not being himself and yet not quite someone else.

Chaliapine died saying, "In what theatre am I?" Such a preoccupation at the moment of leaving life has something sorrowfully tragic. I can conceive of nothing more terrifying than that fantasy of being on a stage at the moment of dying, as if he were still to play another part, as if even his own death did not belong to him.

Explorations into Suffering

Of all forms of human suffering, there is one that seems never to end. It is the agony of finishing with what is finished.

You tell me that E. surmounted his grief in a few months. I do not believe it. It takes years to finish with what is finished. One passes through all the stages of shock and stupor; then comes the recoil and one's astonishment—the refusal to believe, the revolt, the contradictions of flesh and spirit. The body wants to fight, to defend itself; the mind orders silence and the elevation of the problem to a higher level.

In my own case, it was two years after my separation from Maeterlinck before I wakened from my silence and perceived here and there areas of indifference. I could discern in my thought the presence of the irrevocable. I was at last facing the *fact* and I could not stop looking at it. Even at night, in deepest sleep, it remained before me.

Time passes. The next state is long, for it focuses the suffering of deprivation. I began to know which of my amputated habits I was missing most: "I did this, he did that" ... "This is the way I used to speak to him, he would answer me like this" ... Each habit in its turn is a new suffering which informs you of the drama, memory by memory, word by word. In the pain of torn-up roots there is something so strongly terrestrial that suddenly you can no longer look at a flower or a tree. Yet there is an elemental power in this torture that draws you closer to the natural forces; you feel small, yet touched by divinity through the surpassing fact of death—the death of what used to be, what no longer is ... Years pass between the final states of this lethal suffering.

Jealousy

You want me to talk about jealousy? I know only animal jealousy—the kind that is mute. Its manifestations are absurd and insane, but not without a certain grandeur.

Crimes of passion? How absurd juries are with their debates about premeditation, the agony is swift or slow, that is all. When you can speak of it you are not really jealous, when you can weep you are saved. Animal jealousy is stronger than we are. There is no time for a flash of reason. One kills to breathe.

Yesterday I was haunted all day by memories of jealousy . . . I was in a salon, my right hand on the back of a chair. I was looking to the right . . . the thing was happening to the left. He was talking to his mistress—only words, but I was pulled so violently toward them that I no longer felt the hand that was supporting me. My body turned to iron and no longer knew how to walk. I had to move one foot after the other—one, two—walk. A bright stairway, a white marble balustrade, a landing with a chandelier, then steps again. People spoke to me, my lips replied. He had stayed behind with her. All my cells were listening, I could hear what no one else could hear. I was suspended in the realm that separates one from the earth.

Passion

And you want me to talk of passion? Passion which sweeps along in its current so much that is vile, also holds the delicacies of genius. It is the only manifestation of innocence in mankind, what is revolting is the condemnation of passion. We are told to be tolerant of it—what presumption! We are asked to pity, to try to understand. The beauty of passion is that there is nothing to understand, only something to look at and envy. I would be in despair if I had to die without having known this cyclone. I respect it. Passion is the force of acquired speed—an insane race in which you pursue yourself, believing that you are pursuing another. The magnificence of passion is that no human force can stop it.

Ascetics, missionaries, Christian martyrs have all known passion. The world idealizes them without understanding that here is the same force which operates in all people capable of passion, whatever their aim or object. Passion is always immolation; he who kills and he who is killed are equally victims.

The anguish of passion is different from that of jealousy, less intense because more conscious. It is like being burned by a slow fire instead of in a flame. It is a ferocious hunger for the food of happiness, as if one had never eaten. The physical life of the imagination lies herein. If the longed-for delight is distant, inaccessible, one is almost at peace; but to be deprived of it when it is near is to die of hunger before a sumptuous table.

I had not known that I could be so physical . . . I was deprived, and the full moon had come; it hung over its image in the Seine. From the deck of a passing boat came the sound of a waltz. Falling stars slid suddenly across the sky in a rain of light. I wanted to turn away from this insolence of splendors, but I could only lie facing the sky and hold myself rigid, like an animal that is to be operated on.

The Paul Valéry quotation you sent on lust revolts me. I can't imagine this man in love. His mind pleases me and I greatly enjoy his speculations, but how frigid he is! I imagine that he gives even his friendship with a medicine-dropper. Lust is beautiful only if the human animal is beautiful and if he knows how to use his animality beautifully. I dislike the frenzy known as lust—it is always full of false notes, while real passion, when it has measure, is admirable. These two words—passion and measure—seem a contradiction to you? Nevertheless it is from this antithesis that all great things are made. Overflow is never anything but waste. Directed passion is a great orchestral symphony—this is the substance from which a perfect thought of Pascal is molded, as well as every other masterpiece of genius. It is in creative genius that the grandeur of passion can be seen; in life most human beings are too frail to cope with it; this gift of flames from which they should arise, purified, generally leaves them diminished. This fiery gift is greater than the human being who carries it, and whatever is greater than man must be regarded objectively in order not to shrink the materials nature has given him. Objectively I have rarely seen anything as intense as the passion in the film "Karamazoff." It is the story of a cyclone in which man is swept clean, carried out of himself; there remains on the screen only an agony and an indescribable innocence.

Understanding

To understand and to be understood—this was my first great longing. I knew I would never live completely unless it was fulfilled.

Understanding is not the product of dreams. It does not accompany young love with its roses, its frailty, its empty spaces, its ends and its end. My search for it was long and tireless. I began, like everyone else, by believing that I had found it. Like everyone else I saw that I was mistaken and, perhaps not like everyone else, I revised my idea of understanding. Later I saw why it is not easy to come upon. I had hoped to match myself with another's existence when I, myself, did not yet exist.

At twenty I confused understanding with love. I imagined that nothing could unite two people more closely than to share the same ideas, love the same poets, painters, landscapes. I had not yet discovered that, for understanding, it is not necessary to be in love. The understanding that comes from being in love is only a chemical understanding. When it ends, it leaves behind it only sweetness or pain.

Understanding is a sort of love that does not end, because it desires the existence of the loved one as much as its own. I believe it is the only human bond that is not content simply to feed upon its own emotion. It rejects all that can be accepted only if one's eyes are closed, and all that is "impure." In understanding, to lie would be senseless; there are no permissions to be accorded, no commandments to be imposed. Understanding is above tolerance and tests. It is a bond which would not be if it were not perfect.

One cannot have real understanding without a double knowledge—one must know one's self and the other person, one must know the types, categories and tendencies of human beings. I know, for example, that I will never be understood by the "material-world" category. I have nothing in common with those solid friendships which maintain themselves on the every-day plane I abhor. They have something a little concierge about them. Such friends become like two business associates—their strength is doubled but they are not concerned with the quality of their relationship. Of what value is a friendship which does not help you to understand more of yourself, of the other, and of all others?

I look with dismay at people who live together without understanding each other. Everyone says, "But that is natural, life is like that." To me it is as anti-natural as the freaks in the circus.

My first perfect understanding—a pure rapture—was with a poet. A poet never says "It is impossible" or "It is incredible"—he carries within himself a belief in stars, he turns his imagination upon all the earth, the dark of his night is as clear as the light of his day. I never tired of watching Maeterlinck *look* in order to see, *listen* in order to hear. Above all, I lived in the ecstasy of being understood. For the first time someone believed in the fervent substance of my own created world.

On the contrary, I could never have shared my world with a poet like D'Annunzio. His emotional exuberance was such that he fell from a window one day from sheer excitement. I am surprised that his companions didn't jump from their windows in sheer boredom. When we talked in Gardone it was he alone who talked; I was silenced by the knowledge that in the next room, as on a stage set, there stood waiting a mahogany coffin studded with gold. Lack of real life (what I call non-life) consternates me as much in one extreme as in the other—in an ebullition of words or in the ice of silence. D'Annunzio's exuberance, his cries and gesticulations, made me want to flee; but there was something moving in the silence of Maeterlinck, walking in his garden, his face as closed as the book under his arm.

Often I thought I had found understanding, only to realize that the person opposite me was far away—I had been talking all alone. I know now that one cannot create understanding with someone who does not desire it, and a thousand barriers can prevent it even between two people who do desire it. A vice can prevent it—especially a vice like avarice or indelicacy. A too-spherical egoism can prevent it, a slackening of momentum, an ageing of the cells, a lack of good faith, a lack of distinction or a lack of that serious lightness which is so rewarding in human relationships.

I can name any number of tendencies which preclude a relationship of understanding: heavy human vibrations; an empty agitated mind; a ponderous frivolity; people who splash on entering a room as if they were diving; people of sonorous authority whose words clatter like hail against a window; intelligent people whose emanations are impressive but who never speak a word of truth—they approach everything so indirectly that one wonders how they manage to get through a doorway; those talkers with impetuous emanations who push aside everything in their path to make way for their monologues; those people who have no presence at all—their emanations have been clipped off close to their bodies, like shorn sheep; the chronometer people who regulate everything and everyone; and those who strike, who bite, who scratch, who sting, who lie, who eject their venom wherever their anger falls, while their emanations claw and their mouths are pulled into a bitter twist like that of Lugné-Poe.

When I was very young I wrote in my diary: "Great ideas are treated like shelf objects—they are not used. I shall use them." I have kept my word. The great concept contained in "understanding" is what I have always sought, what I have tried to be worthy of, what I have finally found—in the benediction of a true communication with another human being. Ah, if we could only continue to live it for a thousand years!

CHAPTER SEVEN
A STRUGGLE WITH DEATH

PNEUMONIA. It was five o'clock in the evening of the eighth of January 1934 when I was carried away in blankets. The stairway of the Hotel Jacob was old and steep, there was a wide railing, abrupt turnings, sharp corners. I felt very vertical. I was not afraid, I was entering that state of illness which is a state of confident fatalism.

In the ambulance the storm clattered against the window panes. I repeated to myself that pneumonia was a great illness, that I was being taken to a hospital, that perhaps...A nurse waited for me on the steps in the light. I was a bundle that slid about on the stretcher. One flight up, and there was the room— a large room painted grey, with a table, an armchair, two windows—one above the mantelpiece; a long narrow bed without a crease, like polished stone.

It was late when I realized that I was in bed and that Margaret was holding my hands. I suppose I had been talking to myself. Thus I entered into a time which was no longer of the measurement of man. It was reduced to brief instants of lucidity and fantasy in which I heard by chance that I had been in the hospital since the day before. For me barely an hour had passed. I knew that the doctor was standing at the foot of my bed, but I saw no distance between myself and him. I had the feeling that I could take everything into my hands. Life was flat, like a picture.

During the night all things became unbounded and momentous. My body's unused energy—that of all partial deaths—multiplied itself a hundred times. I travelled at top speed through new worlds, my superheated imagination rushed between zero and mad numbers. At zero, it seemed that I was sighing, "I can't go on." But at other moments I dreamed violently that illness is a strange phenomenon—a gaze without distance, a head without size.

Someone was brought in, a voice said, "Here is your nurse, Madame." A person dressed in blue linen was there, her red hands holding an ampule and a syringe. One of her fingers, swathed in white, became as big as a policeman's club. Her eyes aimed at each other and came together to form a single orb; her long donkey teeth bared themselves in a stupid smile, her slow hypodermic tortured me. I had the strength to protest furiously. "A Danish girl," stammered the head nurse, attracted by my cries, "She is very capable." "No, no, she is a Batignolles donkey." But no other nurse could be found—it was a winter of illness.

My doctor, Maurice Delort—that intrepid man who deals with death as if he didn't believe in it—said to me, "I can do nothing without your help. I need you. Don't let yourself go." At this command I emerged from the fatalism of the first hour. A passionate interest can hold life in the plexus of the nerves, like something caught in a net.

From those hours close to death I retain a memory of extreme energy. I felt myself in full action—an activity driven by the will of a body determined to live. The body played the principal part, the great, the only one; and I, spellbound, followed this essential drama without losing a second or a shadow. Cells were fighting. I did not know that the body could be so intelligent.

I think it was the second night. A little black man came running through the window, leaping into the room in the rhythm of a dancing flower. He offered me his services. On other evenings he went quickly from one window to another with a mocking air. Now that I was living in the special region of illness, I understood that he was a ballet master. He was directing a dance of fresh new cells against the deadly movement of microbes.

Standing at the foot of my bed were Doctor Delort and his

two consultants. I could actually see the dynamism of those three men working upon mine, to recall it to life.

I felt a surprising silence, as if life itself were covered with snow. The silence of health is noisy in comparison with this silence which is lined with all that we do not hear. This snowy stillness covered me. I knew it was made of all the dead seconds of my time. They had fallen on me for days.

Sometimes when my hearing returned for a moment, the silence slid from me like an avalanche. I rose and went everywhere, through an understanding so lucid that it was television. I "saw" the old woman of eighty who was in the room above mine, small and grey, she said her rosary softly when they put her in an armchair. And I "saw" a woman in labor in the annex, her black hair in thin strands tossing to her cries and falling about her pallid face.

All my life I have felt the horror of being in a body—a body which will leave me at its hour. Often I have thought: my body will betray me; when my mind perceives the truth for which it longs, it will recognize it, want to capture it, but all in vain—the vision will fade away, my human intelligence will be powerless to follow me into another world . . . I shall depart, abandoning all that was lent to me—a face that will remain on a photograph, a body that contained me, feet that walked the lovely earth. My spirit will go away alone, without belongings, to begin with the seasons its human season. I shall try to be lucid, to take myself up again at the exact point where I shall lose myself today, in order to leave the least possible space between myself and myself. I shall try to follow that impossible following of one's mysterious passage. My nucleus will envelop itself in a new form and take on an appearance which I cannot imagine . . . This idea frightens me, accelerates my blood. I feel it running in my veins at the speed of fountain water.

It is said that at the moment of dying one sees one's whole existence. Memories passed before my eyes as on a cinema screen of which the lower half was completely covered. I saw only the top of events. I would have liked to see some people too, but this was impossible; they were hidden in the shadow.

A single face rose above the darkness. It was the face of Gurdjieff. His mind has marked my own so deeply that there are now only two epochs in my life—the one before him, and the one after him.

What is the phenomenon, life, which none of us knows? Only the prophets knew what it was. They knew life, their life, and living. We would be perfect, like human trees, if this knowledge reached to the end of our branches. As it is, the tree in its sphere manages better than we do.

If I am to live, I swear to myself to go further than before. This oath seems childish, but I do not give myself the right to come out of danger in the same state in which I entered it. I have had the gift of life without understanding its potentialities, and now it is as if a higher justice had taken everything from me in order to force me to understand more. Will I? I believe I shall. The happiness that one sought and found is nothing. One was happy to live it, yet it effaced life. Nothing remains of it. It is a geographical story—a river lost in the sea.

This dying is not terrifying, as one has imagined. It is something new that one does not suspect in the state of living. I know that all the time I made a great effort to understand. The idea of understanding absorbed me, drew all of me into myself.

With all the strength of my being I set myself to watch the core of my being. I did not want it to perish utterly. I worked to detach it from my body. I wanted to tear it out of myself and throw it to it's new beginning so that the perils of the dying body should not reach it.

Now I could scarcely see all that I most adore. I heard the nurse say, "It is noon." But I was talking to the night. It was a simple night, without moon or stars. On the earth the flowers were resting from their colors. I knew them only by their sleeping perfumes.

On the mantelpiece, in front of the window-pane, is a basket of Parma violets, a shutter has been lowered behind it, only at the bottom can I see the light—that miracle. I think of all the people who walk in the daylight seeking—what? Objects, other people. All is mysterious. What must I do to begin to live? Why not die? Because I have done nothing with myself; and because I know there is something to be done. I know all the flaws in the systems of salvation—they start from words, they get lost in words, they end in words. I know that one must give words a body—produce its organs, develop its muscles. Otherwise nothing holds. How can we aspire to survival when we have not known life?

With a great effort I stretched out my arm and drew a hand-kerchief over the luminous hours of my clock, but I knew the hour nevertheless. It was the one that was bound to come, the one that casts a shadow behind the others, the one that awaits its own striking—the hour of life. The hour that is an end is the only one that counts. Each minute contains a complete existence. Minutes are an army in motion, marching toward me.

I wonder if in these hours I really conceived an exact idea of death. Is this possible while one is still in life? I was engaged above all by the great tasks which seemed to me urgent. One of them was to follow a thread in a tangled interminable skein which began before my coming into the world. It was raveled long before me by people I did not know. Generations had tangled and knotted the threads. I worked feverishly, trying to unknot a single one—to know my place of origin, or mark my essence with some guiding sign in order to see, perhaps, my destination.

These were days that I remember with awe. They were not mine alone, I shared them with a succession of circles which opened to me on another plane. I have tried to return there to recapture their meanings, but it is not possible. For me those days were a rehearsal of death. I am moved when I think of this, as if God had given me a special gift; life is like a door a little open since my incursion to the end of the known.

I felt my body dying, but my will remained violently alive. I had already taken leave of the little islands which enclose happiness or unhappiness, pleasure or tears. But I did not have to take leave of love. It was an emotion too essential to die with the body, while I lived my body had participated in the feast of love like a distinguished guest—a guest who even thinks that without his presence there would be no feast. All the senses and their intoxicating enchantment were disappearing, But the approach of death could not break them off cleanly—their bright filaments trailed from the heavens to my bed.

Convalescence

In October I went to Vernet-les-Bains in the Pyrénées-Orientales to recuperate.

The first stage of convalescence is a resurrection; but after that I was placed in a pillory of prohibitions—commanded not to read, write, feel or admire; to do nothing, want nothing, aspire to nothing and above all to be interested in nothing; to communicate no longer with the things about me, to keep the needle of the dial on the word "indifference" and not even to suffer from it; to hold a volume of Rimbaud in my two hands without opening it; to see the moon's reflection on the snow peaks without allowing my heart to quicken; to endure the hours formlessly in one unchanging rhythm until gradually I should begin to live again.

The little box we lived in was only a lid placed on the ground, deep in the country. It was the barest possible existence—a bone of life. Outside my window fountains of willow trees swayed, spraying the sky with brilliant yellow when the wind blew. I had a friendly feeling for the small mountain to the south; it turned green with the rain and told me the time by its pale shadows. Between one and four o'clock I waited for the coming and going of the white bull that passed on the road beside the grey stone wall, his measured tread noble among the disordered rows of cows, his Greek profile raised in obstinacy above the cautious assurance of his step.

In December the great snows came. The villagers told us that more than once the town had been isolated during long winter days—no mail, telegraph or trains. Our box-lid was barely distinguishable from the fields it lay upon. Finally the sun came out and a little bird came in through my open window. He flew to the table where I kept a small fir tree. There he installed himself as if he were at home. I loved his visit and I should have liked to do something charming for him, but we only sat and looked at each other. We remained like that for a long time.

Operation

In the spring we returned to the lighthouse. The forest behind it was full of winged lives and light songs, the river below was gay with rushing tides. One Sunday I came in from the woods, my arms filled with flowers. At the doorstep as I bent down to plunge them into a tub of water, a shock of pain stabbed me and I fainted.

In the morning, at the American Hospital, nurses came to prepare me. My silence was starred with the flowers I had gathered the evening before, I still felt my hands hot among their green stems.

One falls into an illness, one walks into an operation. You could even walk to the execution chamber, but it is customary to be carried there, intact and consenting. My bed was rolled through corridors on rubber wheels. I was in a soundless world, but life there was crude and cruel. I was thinking as one prays. And I realized how ready this silent figure was for pain and the last risk.

The elevator rose to the top floor. There everything was of a dazzling radiance—white masks, white coats, a glass cage in a white sky, and an opaque silence for a rendezvous full of pomp, like a ceremony for an unreal death.

After an operation there is none of that bloom of after-illness when it seems as if a delicate sap were surging in an unknown season. Something deep within you hesitates. Courage again or renouncement? A sort of ancestral cowardice rises and covers life with a dead water. All that constitutes a being, from the first day to the last, is forced into the struggle. One's manner of thinking changes completely. Thought no longer spreads, it runs like a black line on paper.

Later, as danger withdrew, I lost this brevity of thought. All the useless associations and the superfluous speculations returned. I was saved, but restored to habit—to all that we call normal life.

During my struggle with death I had thought, "If I am to live, I swear to myself to go further than before . . . I do not give myself the right to come out of danger in the same state in which I entered it."

And now I was "restored to habit, to normal life" . . . and I was accepting it! A cry of revulsion rose in me, rested petrified in my throat. I sensed that a new cycle of catastrophes would begin if I could not, by a supreme effort, turn my life at last toward its high aim. I must begin to understand better what I already understood, all that the past had taught me in showing me that what is essential lies elsewhere.

This life of mine which in the past had seemed beautiful—had none of it served a purpose? This perfumed wax in which I had modeled my years of art, of love, and of faith in both—was this all that I could contribute to the miracle of a life on earth? No, no, I was ready to step from the present into what would be, at last, the future—that future which is in us and awaits our attention.

CHAPTER EIGHT
A WELL OF WATER

But whosoever drinketh of the water that I shall
give him shall never thirst; but the water that
I shall give him shall be in him a well of water
springing up into everlasting life.

St. John 4, 14

AND so, armed with a supreme resolution, I arrived at that
moment of life which is called descending the other side of
the hill, but which to me is an ascension.

When people reach my age they announce in a tone of curious
satisfaction that they are getting old, their task is done, they can
now relax, it is for others to live. They judge life to be finished
when to me it has barely begun. They see it as a curve, when it
should be an ascending line. To me, life begins at fifty and never
stops growing. All that is worth living begins at that moment, it
is the moment to live "something else."

I have the feeling that I have lived all my life for my particular
present. I must admit that I have not finished with art and moonlight, music and spring, and that I will never be insensible to all
the delights that are the adorable froth of the earth. But these delights are now no longer between my sight and my life. Learning
to "live" demands no startling abdications. It leaves old delights
their place, but not their ancient power. It brings a new purpose,
a new fire, and infinite new ways of seeing all things.

In the last four years I had surmounted three grave illnesses
but I had not yet regained my familiar endless energies. Psychically I had stripped off the tatters of a past that had clung to me
for so long.

Gurdjieff was again in Paris and I was able to see him con-

94

tinually until the war began in 1939. Of that constant association with him, of that work toward "development" which no wellbeing, no happiness, could equal for me, I find it almost impossible to speak.

Many people have investigated doctrines analogous to the Gurdjieff science. To write of them in a word, in a few words, in infinite words, is to deform them—the truth that can enter into a formula is limited. To write abstractly of Gurdjieff conceptions in relation to other great systems of thought, belief, religion, is equally futile. I know the danger of verbalizing over abstract ideas—unless it is to repudiate them. Negations are treated kindly, and the thinker who offers nothing but a hypothesis is always respected. An hypothesis is a life-belt for the mind; thanks to it, the mind floats a little longer before sinking.

I know, too, what the very term "search for truth" suggests of the absurd, the pretentious, the erroneous, the hysterical. Research seems futile. It is less so, however, than to settle one's self comfortably, eyes closed, into a life of which one understands nothing.

And so, in relation to Gurdjieff's doctrine, which became for me "truth," I shall tell simply what I have felt, experienced and understood. I shall not say what I hope from it, but what I have learned to want from it. I shall try to tell what it has done for me in transforming my aspirations into a single and total energy.

In the little red diary which lies before me on my desk I reread the record of what I felt, experienced and understood during those three years. I live again the exaltation and the agony of those daily efforts I made to awaken and develop what was sleeping in me, as in all human beings.

I have copied out some pages of this diary—words written from time to time in the long nights without sleep which became my nights of light.

Diary

Paris, June, 1936. Apartment finally found, rue Casimir Périer, between the church and trees.

Often in pain. Difficult epoch, but marvelous end of month because of my new meeting with Gurdjieff. Went to see him in the Café de la Paix where he always sits before lunch.

"Time passes for me," I said to him, "and I make no progress. I have not many more years to live; will you allow me to read the new parts of your manuscript?"

He looked long at me. At last he said, "You still have time to live. Yes, come to lunch tomorrow and you will read." He murmured words I did not understand. Finally I caught, "You young, but liver sick, all organs blocked." He paused and then said, "Yes, I will do for you." I wanted to cry out my gratitude but I restrained myself, knowing that he understood all I felt. I articulated painfully, "Thank you."

Monday, June 22. Lunched with him, his family and a few pupils in his apartment. After lunch he showed me a little room and a cupboard where he would leave the manuscript for me. He said I might come and read whenever I liked.

Saturday, June 27. Every day I spend two or three hours in his flat. I read with concentration, as if my life depended on the difficult thought that comes from his pages.

Sunday, June 28. Ill again. Couldn't go to read.

Tuesday, June 30. Last night had an acute crisis of pain which involved all the nerves of the solar plexus.* But I shall go to read tomorrow.

---

* This was the last attack.

Thursday, July 16. I am much better. Told Gurdjieff that for the first time in years I have slept through the night. He was glad, and not surprised. He assured me that I would recover, that he had a plan for me, and repeated a second time, "You are young." I understood later that he was referring to my healthy glands. He explained that the first part of the work would take five years, that the body must be strong enough to march with the spirit, because the world of spirit depends on the body which carries it. In Tibet, where he spent so many years of his life, the priests are doctors and the doctors priests.

At lunch he told the others that my case interested him— "She was candidate for death, she is already candidate for life." Then he looked at them with eyes of mischief. "I only said to her, 'Read the book, Madame, read the book.'"

Monday, July 20. What physical amazement when I find I can lie full length on the bed, after so many years of half-reclining; and what astonishment in a body that is dreading pain which does not come. I often feel a great internal heat, as if I were close to a fire. I sleep without waking. I believe that a silent and healing perturbation is taking place in me. I understand what is happening, but to *live* it is unbelievable.

Monday, July 27. Arrived at his flat, dragging myself along. Read the book for three hours. When I left I felt light and strong. Walked two kilometers without weariness. Physically I am living a springtime in this cold month of July. I feel charged like a dynamo.

Thursday, July 30. Gurdjieff came in while I was reading. I was at the end of the chapter on religions. Told him my exaltation in as few words as possible—he doesn't like "manifestations." He was visibly satisfied.

End of August. Never any more pain. I discern something immense that is happening in me. Evidently the brain is not our sole organ of control—other organs also register what takes place in us, and perhaps more accurately than the brain does. I have the impression of a wheel turning within me, motored by a renewed bloodstream and by my conscious will to receive the help given me. I am experiencing the wonderment of something that is not hereditary.

Sunday, September 27. For several months it has been clear that men are unconsciously creating what they call the inevitable—that is, war; and at the same time declaring sincerely that they want only peace.

Wednesday, September 30. Every day I go to study his manuscript, I consider it the authentic event of my life.

The time of destruction—the war—approaches. Yet we work to finish our apartment, which is more and more adorable because of the arched doorways we have constructed throughout. Sooner or later we will lose it.

I have a special anguish as I realize the strength of the energies restored to me. Desires, needs, wishes now assail me, after three years in which I have tried to reconcile myself to the idea of death.

Thursday, October 29. Another period of dark days, since I am no longer tense with perpetual suffering, I feel a curious laxness. And then winter is on the way. My organism follows the uneasiness of the earth beneath its pale colors. The branches of trees make mechanical gestures towards the sky. One's organism has its habits. Because mine has suffered so long it wants to go on suffering, it is more nervous, more sensitive. And I feel myself slipping, I have moments of discouragement. I try not to admit them but they are there nevertheless.

Saturday, October 31. I described my state to him. He already knew and his words brought me comfort, for he made me understand how the law of up-and-down works in all functioning.

Monday, November 2. A great emotion today, when I arrived at Gurdjieff's apartment it was he himself who opened the door. I said immediately, "I am completely well, I am in a new body." The light that came from the little salon illuminated him fully. Instead of avoiding it, he stepped back and leaned against the wall. Then, for the first time, he let me see what he really is . . . as if he had torn off the masks behind which he is obliged to hide himself. His face was stamped with a charity that embraced the whole world. Transfixed, standing before him, I saw him with all my strength and I experienced a gratitude so deep, so sad, that he felt a need to calm me. With an unforgettable look he said, "God helps me."

Wednesday, November 4. From the beginning he has said, "I can prevent pain and therefore prepare the ground for something else." I know that he means a special work, in which the tempo of the spirit will keep pace with the physical recovery. But have I the strength to undertake it?

Wednesday, November 25. Tonight after dinner Gurdjieff played his little accordion-piano. Unique spectacle. This is the man who says, "I try to be a man without quotation marks." As he played one saw a man live—as complete as a circle. And the richness of his smile! Richness of bounty, richness of truth.

Christmas Eve. Extraordinary reunion at his flat tonight. Another age—a patriarch distributing treasures. The little apartment was full—his family, friends of his family, the concierge and his family, old servants from other days. The Christmas tree, too big, too high, was bent against the ceiling and its stars hung down.

The distribution of gifts was a true ceremony. Fifty or more large boxes, numbered, occupied a corner of the salon. Gurdjieff, standing in front of a table, glasses on his nose, held a list in his hand. To each box that was set before him he added notes of a hundred or five hundred francs; then he called a name corresponding to a number and presented the box, making a brief gesture that signifies "Don't thank me." The last to come forward was a Danish doctor who received a handsome dressing-gown and a thousand-franc note. As Gurdjieff placed the money in the box, S. said, "He's going to be happy, that one." Gurdjieff answered like lightning, "Not you?"

At ten o'clock supper was served. On each plate was an enormous piece of mutton, a stuffed Russian roll, pickles, peppers preserved in oil—all the things I hold in horror; but superb desserts were spread out—cakes, fruits, candies of a thousand-and-one-nights. We left at midnight and other people took our places. The Russian maid said to me, "From one o'clock till dawn the poor will be coming."

We know that for him a period of fasting will follow this feast, to balance so many days of abundance.

Wednesday, December 30. Resurrection . . . absorbing and primordial question for me—the successive deaths and the perpetual renewals of life: addition of what was, what is, and what will be. A new kind of resurrection begins in me—I am invaded by the all-powerfulness of spirit. This surpasses life itself.

Thursday, December 31. If I am able to understand Gurdjieff a little in his entirety, it is because I have studied him and his doctrine for over twelve years. One of his greatest virtues is knowing how to render intelligible to human understanding the truths that are the most impossible for the mind of man to conceive.

My intelligence—no, I don't value it; and anyway, in these matters, intelligence moves into second place. What I have always valued in myself is not my intelligence but a fundamental lucidity which has never failed me in all the disasters of my existence. Before my experience with Gurdjieff I saw the time approaching when this lucidity alone would be left in me, like a flag on an empty house.

My notes from January, 1937, to the following December show only long months of effort—the climbing and falling known to all those who have tried to follow the difficult "road of knowledge."

But what does this vague phrase, road of knowledge, mean? Philosophers claim that all knowledge can be found within four walls, in books. Yet everyone can read Hermes, Pythagoras, Buddha, the Bible, and remain blind before these inscrutable codes. It is not enough to read, admire, speculate. The study of "Know thyself" demands a special work and a life given up to it. One must begin the work. What one has learned, one must incorporate. The time that stretches between these two states is full of panic. But all initiation holds a period of panic, just as all work holds within it the same laws: the road which at first appears to be vertical becomes less steep as one climbs.

Some of the pages of my diary during this period are almost incoherent with despair. At other moments I had no despair, neither had I hope. I was living in a tunnel. Then on the tenth of October I wrote:

I know that I am approaching a momentous state. I know the balance I must maintain in all the coming tests, and some lines of Goethe haunt me: "No path! It is the jungle that one cannot penetrate... And then in the eternally empty distance you will see nothing, you will not hear the sound of your foot-steps, you will have nothing upon which to rest . . ."

I know this and I detest my anguish. However great it is I judge it to be small. Yet I am afraid—a thousand fears which have no name. It is my parents, my ancestors, who are afraid in me. Why listen to their fears? I was not so afraid when I faced death. Was that, then, more natural? Yes.

Others before me have done what I am doing. But that does not help me—each person's experience is different. I envy those who plunge in without hesitating. I am ashamed of my hesitation, I seem to be bargaining. A small life for a great truth—I must choose. Yet I want to discuss the choice with myself before I give up this self to its task. I will advance in darkness; "seeing" will be abolished for the sake of "being." The hardest moment of all will arrive. The guide will watch me stumble, exhaust myself, and will say nothing. His words were: "I cannot develop you. I can create conditions in which you can develop yourself."

Tuesday, October 12. I had a dream. I walked for years, search-ing a planet. Across space I arrived. At first I thought that the cities, the people, the things, were like ours. Soon I saw that all was different. People loved one another and they did not speak. The animals spoke.

I had a long conversation with a white horse as large as a cathedral. He explained his two-dimensional vision and his terrors. He understood that I was burning and to relieve me he hung his mane like a rain about my body. It was he who explained the celebration of a festival such as does not exist in our world. Three seasons had conquered the fourth. I watched the triumphant return of the troops—regiments of all the countries advanced, flag flying, followed by spring times and early autumns. They had killed the winters.

They were not accompanied by good and evil. Their songs

were bells, their laughter was like the sunlit sea. To amuse themselves along the way they had disciplined plagues, abolished pain, hunted down calumny. My companion said, "With winter dead, they have killed the inevitable. Now death will be no more than a result—the consequence of not having understood."

Suddenly one of the men fell from high up on to the ground before me. He split in two. He was empty.

Monday, October 18. The important moment is here, my choice has been made. Tomorrow we will ask Gurdjieff—Margaret and I—whether the time has come for us to begin our real work.

When I really begin, nothing will have changed in appearances. I will still have my name that I do not like, I will be dressed as I am now. I will go tomorrow morning and simply say to Gurdjieff, "I will do." Just these three words, but for me, before myself, they will be the authentic beginning of my life. When I say these words I will see before me a succession of unknown experiences which I will pass through, without perceiving the end. My end, I believed, would be my death. Now there comes an end before the end, a death before my death. And it is to win a life.

Tuesday, October 19. Five o'clock in the morning, in my room, Casimir Périer. The sky is pale blue behind the still trees. All is happy and calm, why, why, did I have to learn that one can live beyond this easy, lovely human life? I loved that life . . .

At eleven o'clock Margaret and I will ask Gurdjieff to begin.

. . . *Later.* He has agreed, and given us a rendezvous at his flat tomorrow at one.

Wednesday, October 20. As soon as we arrived he explained again all that we already knew: the need to be sure; to realize that the work would become more and more difficult; that it was not too late to say "no." He didn't speak of rewards. The first for me is that he wants us to work together, helping each other.

Thursday, October 21, late afternoon. Divine weather in the Luxembourg Gardens, with whirling dead leaves. I sat on a bench near the fountain and thought about the new work Gurdjieff had explained this morning in a manner so clear, so total, that I understood it without understanding all his words. For me it is the long-awaited revelation, so real that it has infinite repercussions in my being.

Many years ago—it may be forty—I wrote to Maeterlinck: "I do not know if you understand me—I am comparable to a bubble that floats in the air and is attached to nothing real; even in the depths of myself I feel that I *am not*. One single preoccupation, perhaps, exists in this void—it is my anxiety at seeing myself thus; and, as if to change, I must accomplish something unknown. It comes from very far in me, like a lost idea, a commandment to which I can give no form; and I search, I search . . ."

Today, a life later, now that I have found at last what one can *do*, I see again those words, "As if, to change, I must accomplish something unknown."

Eleven o'clock at night. Today, this 21st of October, 1937, I have lived a few real moments.

End of December. I am living too hard, I am tired, my sleep is made of paper.

If at this moment I saw death approaching, I would not accept it as I did in the hospital beds where I spent so many months. How my time is heavy with a true abundance of which I never dreamed.

I said to Gurdjieff, "I am almost afraid—life rises in me like the sea." He repeated, "It is only a small beginning."

The Lighthouse, Summer, 1938

Now that I have collected my notes written during my "change of course," I am struck by an essential paradox which I find hard to understand. What was that anguish, that despair, which was in me and yet so far from me? It took place so far from my lived life that it never had a voice, not one audible cry. Why that pain when I had no pain? Is "the soul," then, really elsewhere? I did not know it had to suffer so to beget itself. Since it is my life, how could it have been so outside my human days?

I write these words in the circle of a flashlight, in order not to disturb the two sleepers who might see a glow in my room and think me ill. I had been sleeping after assembling my notes, this afternoon and all evening. Now it is night—three o'clock in the morning. Through the window the moon and its reflection in the water touch my bed . . . I was asleep and suddenly my sleep was torn in two by an idea: where did that despair of which I wrote take place, when my life was so happy? . . . The circle of light falls clearly on my notebook, I hear the silky pulsation of a passing boat, a red glow moves across the ceiling . . . I have lived for years in the shadow of a deep preoccupation which, however, clarified me and uncovered many things to my sight. Is it that my subconscious has its own life which does not identify itself with mine? Mine could be in peace while the other was living its own personal drama? That drama is like a love that has no name, no face, and that struggles perpetually to take a form, to *be* and to give being to someone. That someone was I, who did not know it.

Le Cannet, Alpes Maritimes, 1940

CPSIA information can be obtained
at www.ICGtesting.com
Printed in the USA
BVOW03*0822281017
498338BV00004BA/22/P